EYEWITNESS

HURRICANE & TORNADO

Cyclone shelter

Spots on the Sun

Sunset at Stonehenge, England

19th-century reproduction of Galileo's thermoscope

Saturn

Lighthouse at the George Washington Bridge in New York

Wind-eroded rocks in Arizona

EYEWITNESS

HURRICANE & TORNADO

WRITTEN BY
JACK CHALLONER

Simultaneous waterspout and lightning bolt

Storm chasers observing a supercell storm

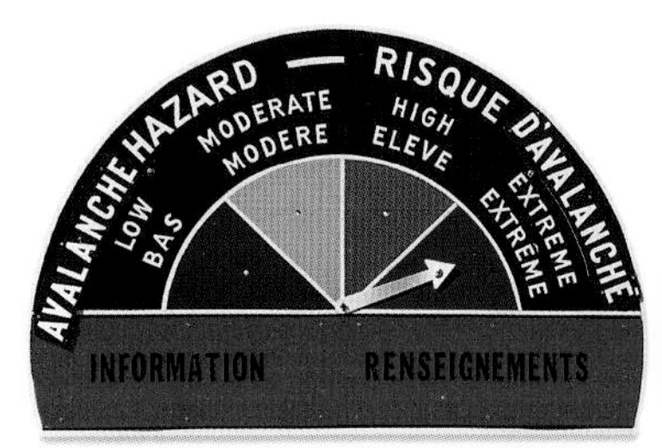

Avalanche warning sign

REVISED EDITION

DK LONDON
Senior Editor Carron Brown
Senior Art Editor Lynne Moulding
US Editor Kayla Dugger
US Executive Editor Lori Cates Hand
Managing Editor Francesca Baines
Managing Art Editor Philip Letsu
Senior Production Editor Andy Hilliard
Production Controller Samantha Cross
Senior Jackets Designer Surabhi Wadhwa-Gandhi
Jacket Design Development Manager Sophia MTT
Publisher Andrew Macintyre
Associate Publishing Director Liz Wheeler
Art Director Karen Self
Publishing Director Jonathan Metcalf

Consultant Sam Hardy

DK DELHI
Senior Editor Shatarupa Chaudhari
Senior Art Editor Vikas Chauhan
Editor Shambhavi Thatte
Art Editor Baibhav Parida
Picture Researcher Vishal Ghavri
Managing Editor Kingshuk Ghoshal
Managing Art Editor Govind Mittal
DTP Designers Nand Kishor Acharya, Pawan Kumar, Rakesh Kumar
Jacket Designer Juhi Sheth

FIRST EDITION
Project Editor Melanie Halton **Art Editor** Ann Cannings
Managing Editor Sue Grabham
Senior Managing Art Editor Julia Harris
Editorial Consultant Lesley Newson
Picture Research Mollie Gillard, Samantha Nunn
DTP Designers Andrew O'Brien, Georgia Bryer
Production Kate Oliver

This Eyewitness ® Book has been conceived by Dorling Kindersley Limited and Editions Gallimard

This American Edition, 2021
First American Edition, 1995
Published in the United States by DK Publishing
DK, 1745 Broadway, 20th Floor, New York NY 10019

22 23 24 25 10 9 8 7 6 5 4 3
004–314303–Dec/2021

A catalog record for this book is available from the Library of Congress.
ISBN 978-0-7440-3964-1 (Paperback)
ISBN 978-0-7440-2895-9 (ALB)

Printed and bound in China

For the curious
www.dk.com

This book was made with Forest Stewardship Council™ certified paper–one small step in DK's commitment to a sustainable future.
For more information go to www.dk.com/our-green-pledge

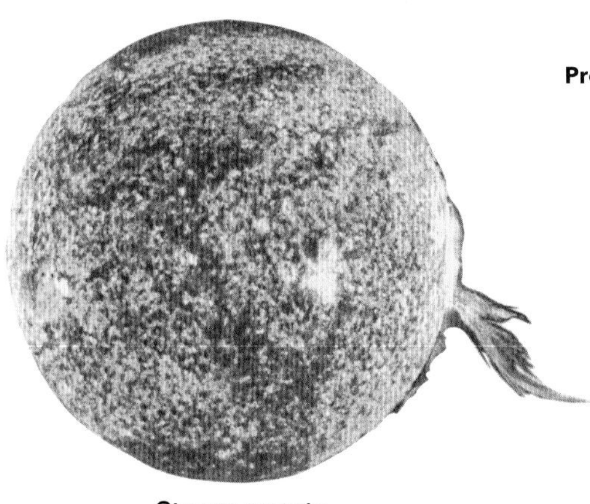
Storm erupts on the Sun

Mount St. Helens erupting

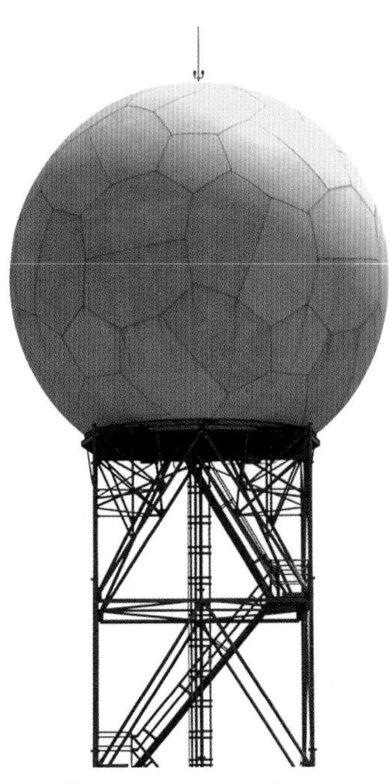
Doppler-radar dome

Hurricane warning flags

Storm system viewed from space

Contents

Icicle formation in Arizona

Weather **folklore**

In ancient times, people didn't know how the weather worked. Some realized that clouds were made of water, but they did not understand the wind or the Sun. Many believed the gods made the weather; others observed plants, animals, or the sky to work out a forecast. Some of these observations were reliable, but an accurate forecast requires a full understanding of how the weather works. Weather science was begun by philosophers in ancient Greece, but they did not test their theories, so they were often wrong.

Magic charms

This figurehead from the Solomon Islands would have been on the front of a canoe to ward off dangerous storms at sea. Many lucky charms that are used to protect people against bad weather are linked to gods or spirits.

Sun worship

Throughout history, many cultures have worshipped the Sun. Stonehenge in England is thought to be an ancient place of Sun worship. Some stones line up to where the Sun rises on the summer solstice (when the Sun is at its highest).

Weather sacrifice

Legend says that the Mayan rain god Chac sent rain for crops, but also storms, which destroyed crops. People made offerings to Chac to keep the rains but stop the storms.

EYEWITNESS

Scientific thinkers

Ancient Greek philosophers Aristotle and Plato were among the first people to try to explain scientifically how the weather works, including cloud, hail, storm, and snow formation, plus Sun halos. Their ideas were very influential and were not challenged for about 2,000 years.

Italian fresco from 1511 showing Plato (left) and Aristotle (right)

Sky watching

An ancient Maori myth describes Tawhaki, the god of thunder and lightning, going up to the sky disguised as a kite. Maori priests believed they could predict the weather by flying kites and watching how they moved across the sky.

Maori kite made of canvas and twigs

Furry tale

Some people believe that the bushier a squirrel's tail is during fall, the harsher the winter will be. There is no scientific evidence for this.

Bushy-tailed squirrel

Stormy tale

In the Shinto religion, divine being Amaterasu Omikami lights up heaven. Her brother, a storm god, causes strong winds and floods, which make Amaterasu hide in a cave and the world go dark—just like during a storm.

The Stonehenge was erected in stages from about 3100 BCE

Each of the blocks in Stonehenge weighed 33 tons (30 tonnes).

Animal forecast

Many animals respond to changes in temperature, humidity, or atmospheric pressure. Roosters often crow before a thunderstorm. Observing animals can help with weather forecasts.

Cone watch

Pine cones open their scales in dry air and close them when it is humid. Air is normally humid before rainfall, so pine cones can help forecast wet weather.

Rain cry

These Yali tribesmen of New Guinea are performing a dance to call for rain. Dancers carry grass, which is believed to pierce the eye of the Sun and makes it cry tears of rain.

Early **forecasts**

Meteorology, or modern weather science, began about 300 years ago, when people started to experiment scientifically with water, heat, and air—the components of weather. They learned about atmospheric pressure and invented measuring devices, including the barometer (measures atmospheric pressure) and the thermometer (measures temperature). These early developments gradually led to a better understanding of the atmosphere's physical mechanisms in the 20th century. Today, powerful computers and satellites help predict weather accurately many days in advance.

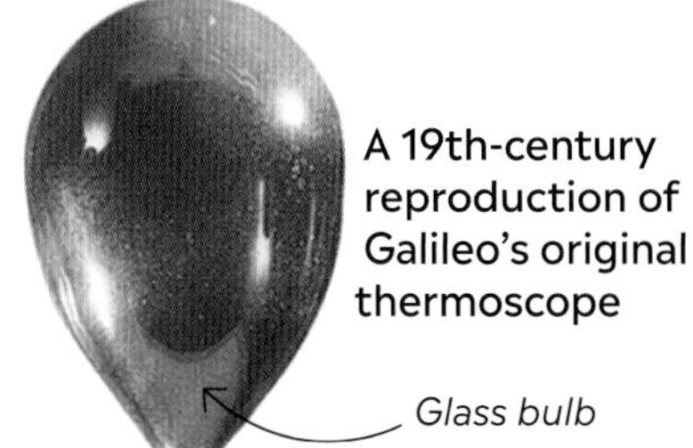

A 19th-century reproduction of Galileo's original thermoscope

Glass bulb

High temperature

Italian physicist Galileo Galilei designed this thermoscope (early thermometer) about 400 years ago. A long tube with a bulb at the end sat in a flask of water. As the temperature rose, air in the bulb expanded, causing the water level in the tube to drop. As it became cooler, the air contracted and the water level rose.

Flask would have been filled with water

Hotness scale

When this thermometer was made in 1657, there was no agreed scale for reading measurements. Today, meteorologists use two main scales to record temperature—Fahrenheit and Celsius. Both scales were invented in the 18th century.

An eye on the storm

Cyclonic winds spiral at their center, and so, before hurricane radio warnings, sailors used this barocyclonometer to measure changes in wind direction and atmospheric pressure. They could then work out which way the hurricane was moving and steer their vessels to safety.

Thick needle aligns with the normal path of storms in the region

Thin needle indicates safe course away from the storm

Invisible water

Air normally becomes humid (contains more water) before a thunderstorm. The water in the air is an invisible vapor, but a hygrometer, designed about 350 years ago, is able to measure it. Water is absorbed from the air by the cotton bag, which becomes heavier. The greater the humidity, the more the bag drops down.

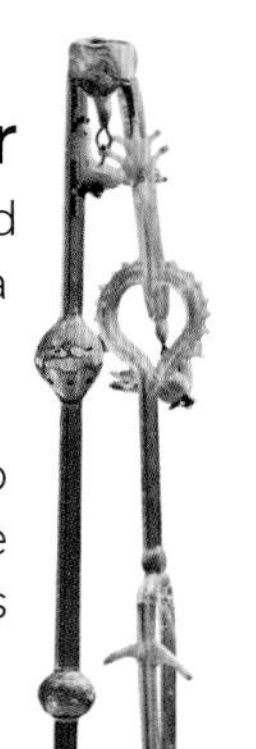

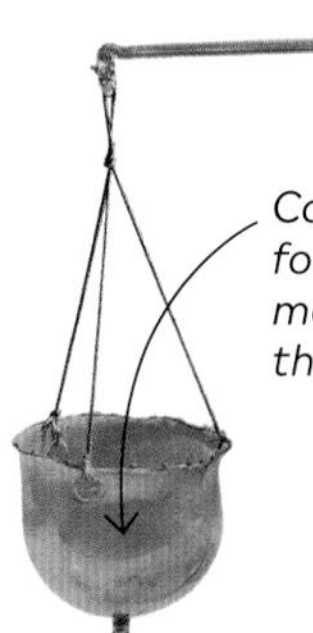

17th-century balance hygrometer

Cotton bag for absorbing moisture in the air

Balancing weight made of glass

EYEWITNESS

Early forecaster
Norwegian meteorologist Vilhelm Bjerknes (1862–1951) used his knowledge of physics to understand the workings of Earth's atmosphere. He developed groundbreaking ideas, including formulas that are still used today for weather analysis and forecasts.

Moving mercury

Meteorologist Robert Fitzroy invented this barometer, which has a scale to measure the mercury column. Fine weather is forecast when atmospheric pressure pushes the mercury column above 30 in (76 cm); unsettled weather is predicted when it falls below this.

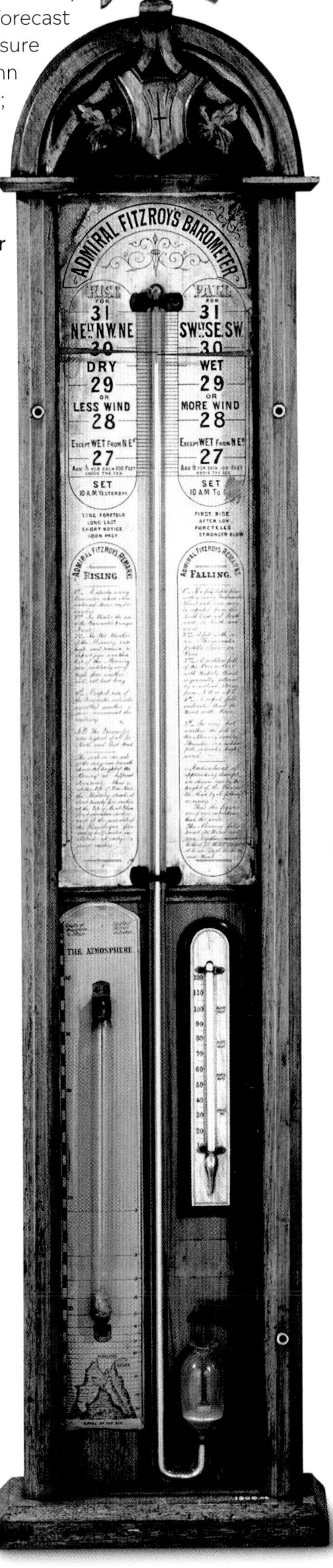

Fitzroy barometer

Under pressure

In 1643, Italian physicist Evangelista Torricelli made the first barometer—a 3-ft (1-m) long tube filled with mercury and put upside down in a bowl of mercury. The weight, or pressure, of air on the mercury in the bowl stopped the mercury in the tube from falling below 30 in (76 cm).

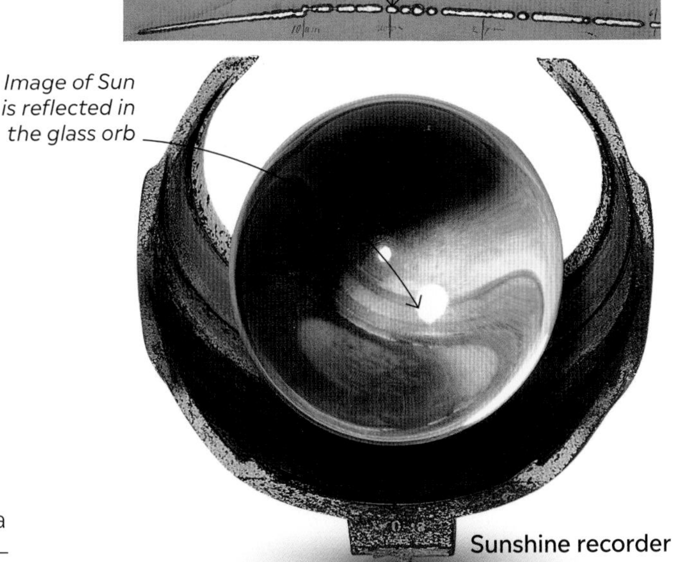

Sunshine recorder

Focused measurement

This glass ball focuses sunlight to scorch paper. As the Sun moves across the sky, the trail of scorches shows the amount of sunlight. If clouds hide the Sun, there is not enough direct sunlight to scorch paper.

NUMERICAL MODELING

Nowadays, we can produce climate models—computerized representations of the atmosphere based on a 3D global grid. These models take our best estimate of the current weather and solve complicated mathematical equations to predict the future weather.

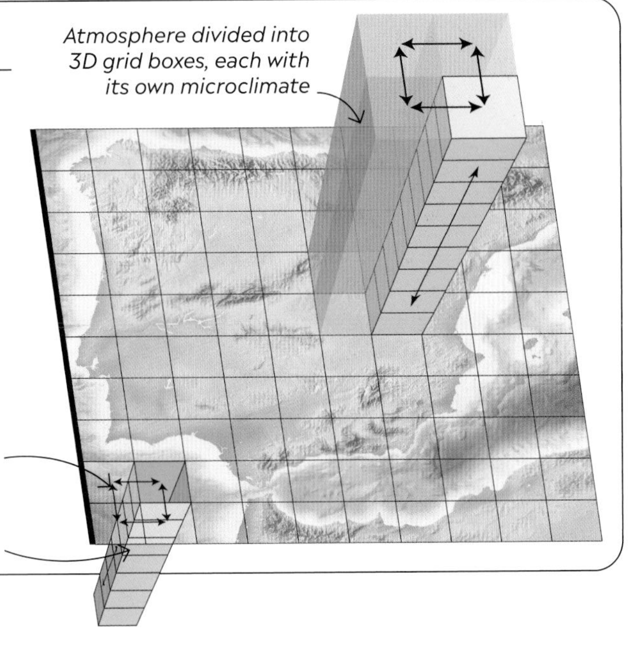

What is **extreme weather?**

From hurricanes and tornadoes, to droughts and floods, to freezing and high temperatures, extreme weather can be dangerous. Weather can be described by wind speed, temperature, atmospheric pressure, and precipitation (rain, hail, or snow). The average world temperature is 59°F (15°C), but some places are colder or warmer. The average rainfall is 39 in (100 cm) per year, but some places have no rain, while others have too much and all at once. Extreme weather can happen where weather is usually calm.

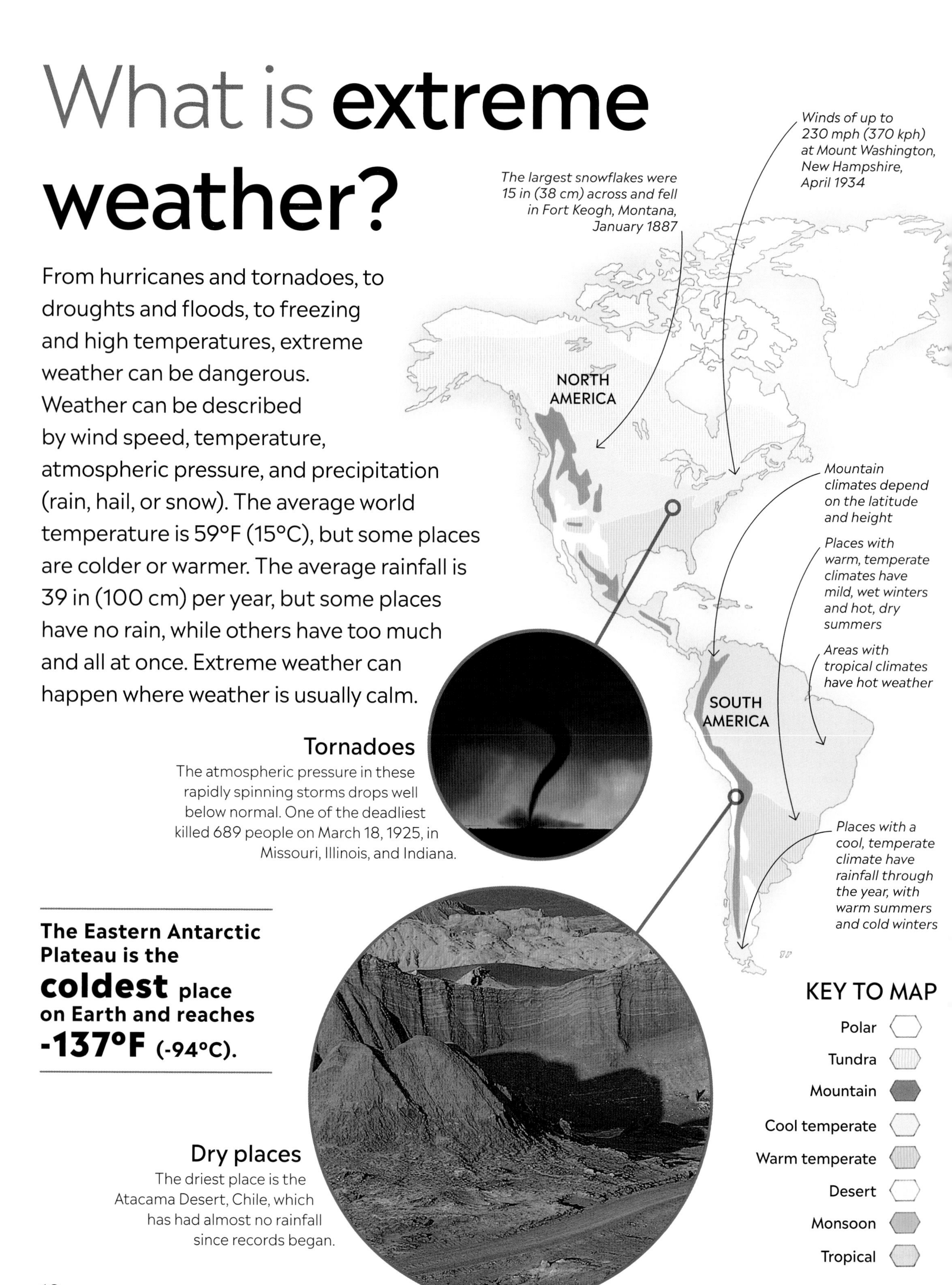

Tornadoes

The atmospheric pressure in these rapidly spinning storms drops well below normal. One of the deadliest killed 689 people on March 18, 1925, in Missouri, Illinois, and Indiana.

The Eastern Antarctic Plateau is the coldest place on Earth and reaches -137°F (-94°C).

Dry places

The driest place is the Atacama Desert, Chile, which has had almost no rainfall since records began.

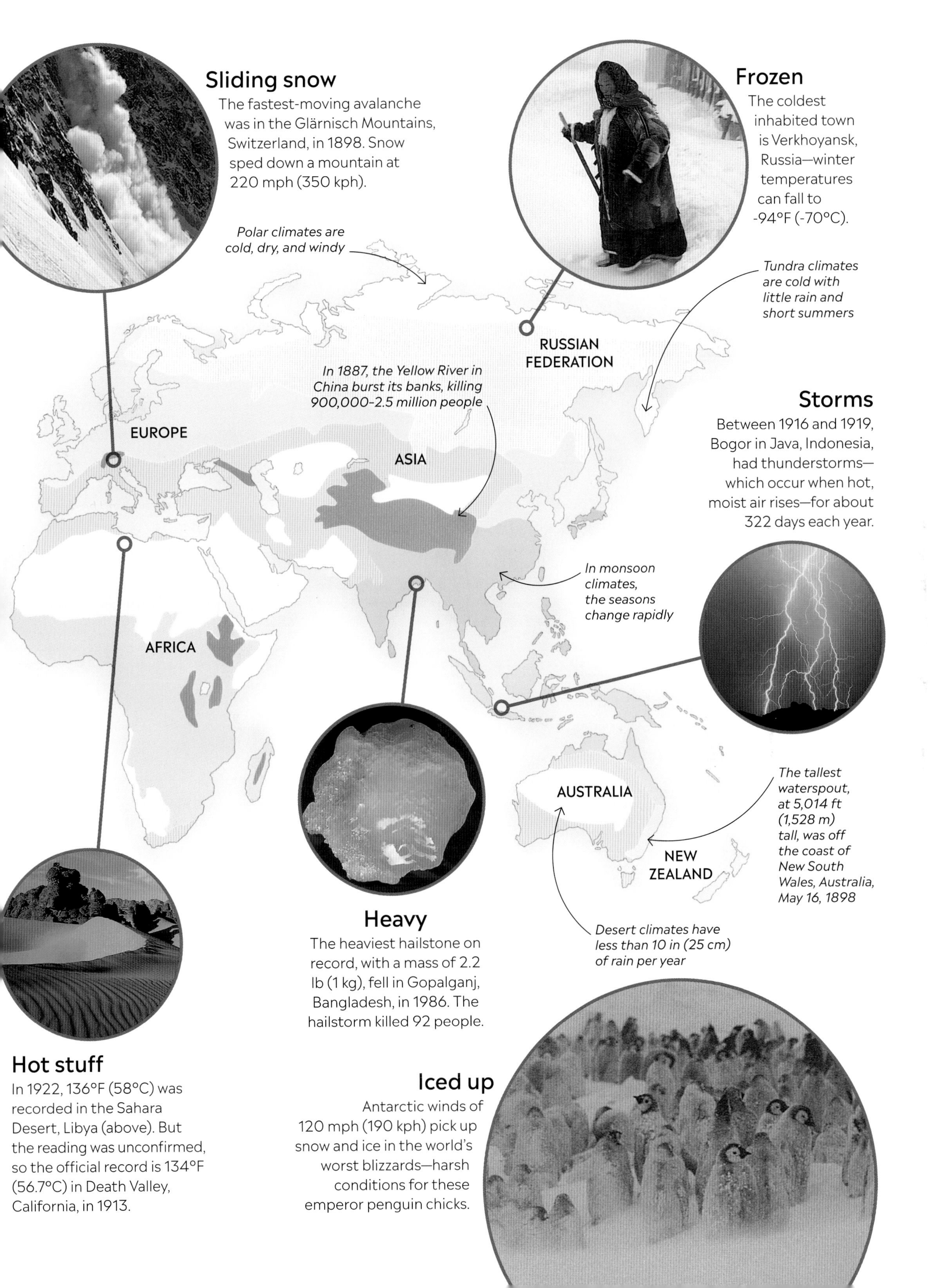

Sliding snow

The fastest-moving avalanche was in the Glärnisch Mountains, Switzerland, in 1898. Snow sped down a mountain at 220 mph (350 kph).

Frozen

The coldest inhabited town is Verkhoyansk, Russia—winter temperatures can fall to -94°F (-70°C).

Storms

Between 1916 and 1919, Bogor in Java, Indonesia, had thunderstorms—which occur when hot, moist air rises—for about 322 days each year.

Heavy

The heaviest hailstone on record, with a mass of 2.2 lb (1 kg), fell in Gopalganj, Bangladesh, in 1986. The hailstorm killed 92 people.

Hot stuff

In 1922, 136°F (58°C) was recorded in the Sahara Desert, Libya (above). But the reading was unconfirmed, so the official record is 134°F (56.7°C) in Death Valley, California, in 1913.

Iced up

Antarctic winds of 120 mph (190 kph) pick up snow and ice in the world's worst blizzards—harsh conditions for these emperor penguin chicks.

Extreme **causes**

Important factors that affect the weather include the Sun heating Earth and differences in atmospheric pressure. Other factors include dust from volcanoes and storms on the Sun's surface, which can make it hotter or colder, or wetter or drier. Pollution in the atmosphere also affects the weather. Causes of extreme weather are understood, but predicting weather more than a few days ahead is still impossible, because the weather is a complex and sensitive system.

Global warming

Many gases and smoke particles from modern industry hang in the air. This can affect the weather. Carbon dioxide from fossil fuels is contributing to an increase in the world's temperature. This "global warming" could upset weather balances, bringing more storms and rising sea levels.

Harmful gases

Chlorofluorocarbons (CFCs) are released by industrial processes and—until the 1990s, when they were banned—by aerosol cans. CFCs break down ozone—a gas in Earth's atmosphere. Ozone protects Earth from harmful ultraviolet radiation. CFCs are known as "greenhouse gases," as they slowly increase the world's temperature.

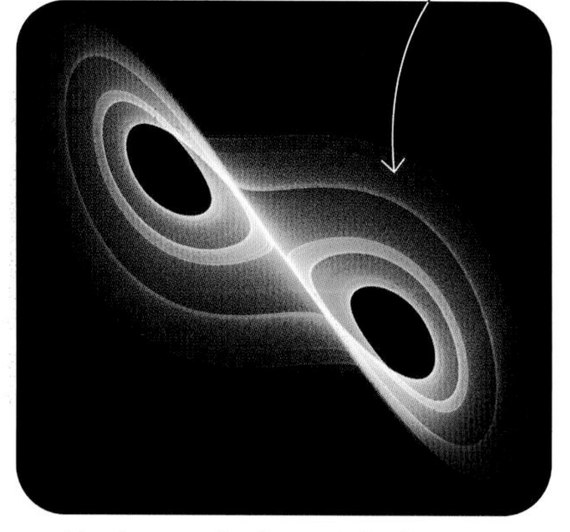

Mathematical model of chaos theory from Lorenz's data

Chaotic weather

According to chaos theory (the study of unpredictable systems), a slight change in air movement in one location, such as the flap of a butterfly's wings, can alter the course of the weather elsewhere. Mathematician Edward Lorenz discovered the chaotic behavior of the atmosphere in the 1960s. His findings led to improvements in weather forecasting.

HOT AND COLD

The Sun is Earth's main energy source. Sunlight hits the poles at an angle due to Earth's shape, so the poles have less intense heat than at the equator. These temperature differences alter atmospheric pressure, causing global winds that influence weather patterns.

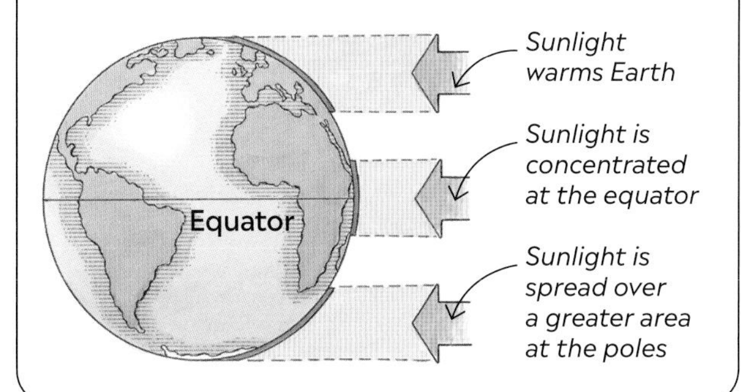

Global cooling

Mount St. Helens in Washington erupted in 1980. For a few months after, there was a drop of 1°F (0.5°C) in the average global temperature due to volcanic dust blocking some of the Sun's heat and light.

Spotting bad weather

Dark, cool patches can appear on the Sun's surface for about a week. These sunspots throw out debris that sometimes reaches Earth. The spots are most numerous every 11 years, and extreme weather on Earth seems to coincide with this cycle.

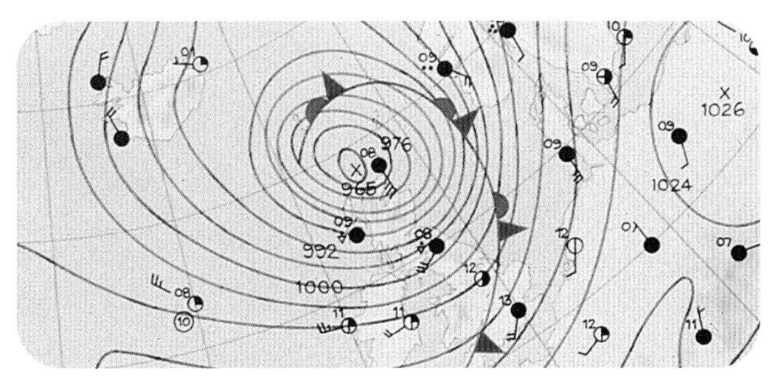

Deep depression

This synoptic chart shows a depression—a common feature of unsettled weather—over the British Isles. A depression, or an area of low pressure, forms when air near the surface converges, rises, and cools. Winds spiral in toward the center. Severe weather is often focused near boundaries between warm and cold air known as fronts.

Severe **winds**

Strong winds can wreak havoc. Their force depends on their speed. The fastest winds at ground level are in hurricanes and tornadoes; higher in the atmosphere are even faster winds—jet streams—that help distribute the Sun's heat around the world. Global winds are caused by the Sun heating parts of the Earth differently, while local winds are caused by regional changes in temperature and pressure.

Head faces in the direction from which the wind is blowing

Weather vane

Weather vanes are perhaps the oldest meteorological instruments. This weathercock's tail swings around as the wind changes direction and points the head toward the wind. A reading is taken of where the wind blows from.

The windy city

Chicago, Illinois, is on Lake Michigan, where inland and lake air mix. During the warm season, inland Chicago heats up faster than the lake. Cool air over the lake flows inland as a lake breeze, keeping temperatures lower.

Flying in the wind

In March 1999, balloonists Bertrand Piccard and Brian Jones became the first to fly a hot-air balloon nonstop around the world. Their balloon, Breitling Orbiter 3, was sometimes assisted by jet-stream winds, blowing up to 186 mph (300 kph).

Standing tall

This model shows the 2,755-ft (840-m) tall Millennium Tower that was proposed for Tokyo, Japan. A skyscraper needs wind resistance. This tower is encircled by a steel frame for strength and protection from winds.

Wind swept

Wind and sand erosion has carved these sandstone rocks. If severe winds blow across the rocks, sweeping up sand, dense and dangerous sandstorms may occur.

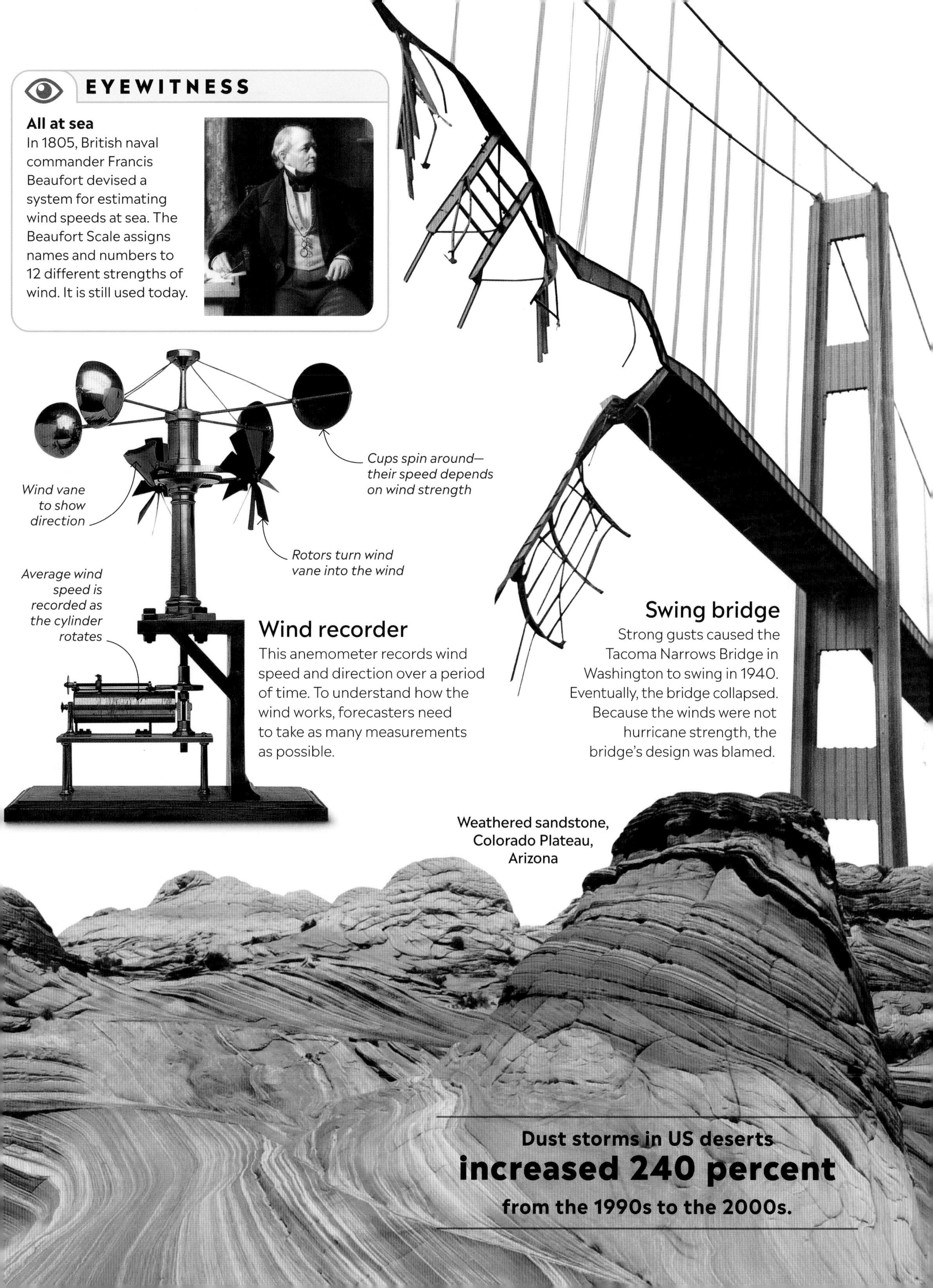

EYEWITNESS

All at sea

In 1805, British naval commander Francis Beaufort devised a system for estimating wind speeds at sea. The Beaufort Scale assigns names and numbers to 12 different strengths of wind. It is still used today.

Wind recorder

This anemometer records wind speed and direction over a period of time. To understand how the wind works, forecasters need to take as many measurements as possible.

Swing bridge

Strong gusts caused the Tacoma Narrows Bridge in Washington to swing in 1940. Eventually, the bridge collapsed. Because the winds were not hurricane strength, the bridge's design was blamed.

Weathered sandstone, Colorado Plateau, Arizona

Dust storms in US deserts increased 240 percent from the 1990s to the 2000s.

Thunderous **storms**

Huge amounts of energy are released in the rain, winds, thunder, and lightning that accompany thunderstorms. The most energetic storms create hail or tornadoes. The source of energy is the Sun, which causes water to evaporate; the resulting warm, moist air rises and cools, creating a cumulonimbus cloud. The rising current of air (an updraft) may travel more than 60 mph (100 kph). When rain or hail falls, a downdraft of cooler air causes gusty winds.

Water carrier

A thunderhead is a towering cumulonimbus cloud. It may reach a height of 7.5 miles (12 km), while its base may loom just 3,280 ft (1,000 m) above ground. It usually contains about 11,023 tons (10,000 tonnes) of water.

Supercell

Most thunderstorms begin as cells (pockets) of rising air. A "supercell" is a very large, long-lived, energetic cell in which the entire thunderstorm is rotating. Supercells create dangerous hazards, including tornadoes, torrential rain, and damaging hail.

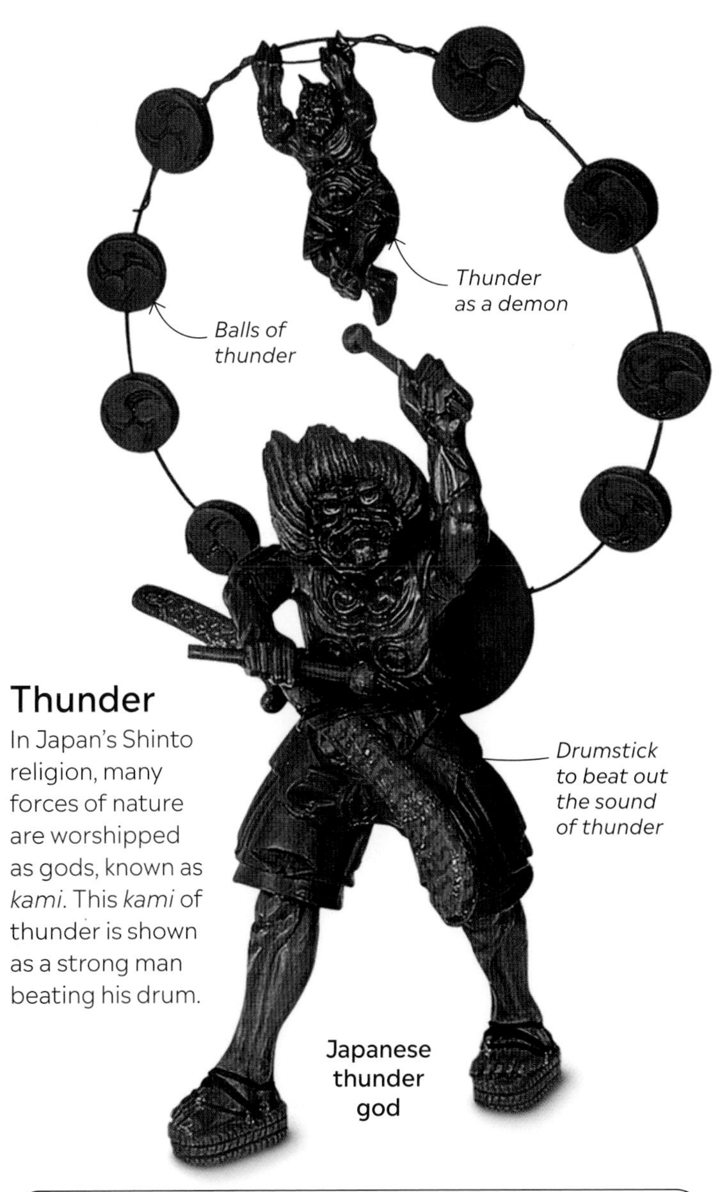

Japanese thunder god

Thunder

In Japan's Shinto religion, many forces of nature are worshipped as gods, known as *kami*. This *kami* of thunder is shown as a strong man beating his drum.

View from the air

This photograph, taken from a spacecraft orbiting Earth, shows how a system of storms can develop when cold, dry air undercuts warm, moist air, lifting it to form pockets of rising air. These pockets show up as thunderheads.

Letting go

Tornadoes, lightning, and waterspouts often occur during severe storms as thunderclouds quickly release energy.

LIFE OF A STORM

A thunderstorm develops when an updraft (red arrows) of warm, moist air forms a cloud as the moisture evaporates from the air. Water vapor releases heat as it condenses. This heat warms the air more and causes it to rise higher. The storm subsides when the air cools, and the downdraft (green arrows) disperses the cloud.

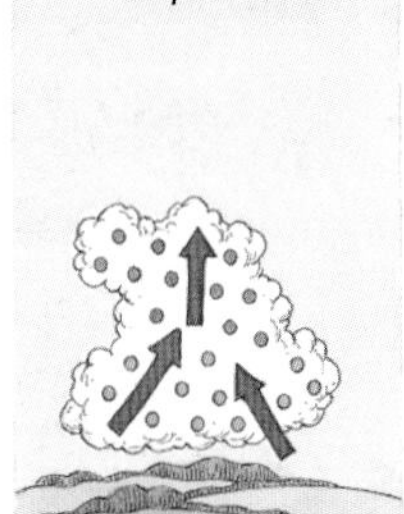

Hot, moist air rises

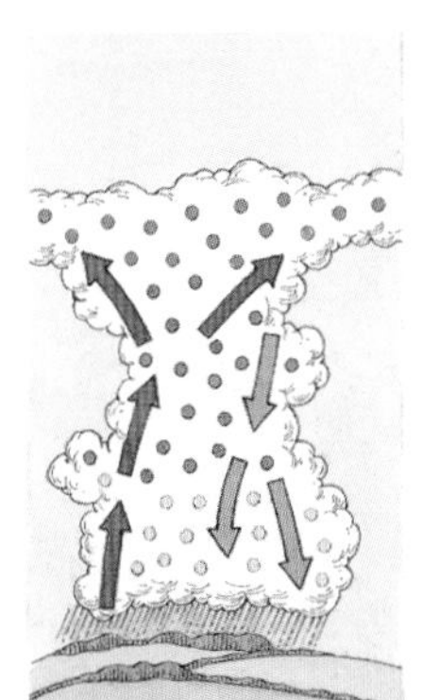

Heavy rain and hail

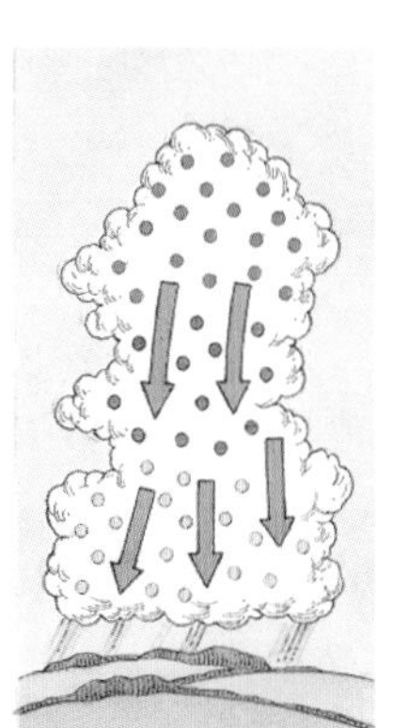

Cloud runs out of energy

Summer storms

Thunderstorms often occur after a hot day, when air warmed by the ground rises quickly into cooling air. Dense thunderclouds absorb almost all the light that falls on them. This is why they appear black.

Twisting **tornadoes**

Tornadoes have many names, including whirlwinds and twisters. These high-speed spiraling winds leave a trail of destruction and are a bit of a mystery. They seem to develop at the base of thunderclouds as warm, moist air rises and passes through colder air. Somehow this draws winds that are already circulating the storm into a high-speed whirl. The pressure at a tornado's center is lower than outside, creating a funnel that sucks up anything in its path.

Liquid funnel

A waterspout is a rotating column of air over a body of water. Unlike tornadoes, most waterspouts are not associated with severe thunderstorms and move very slowly. Occasionally, however, they can form in the same way as tornadoes and cause significant damage.

A tornado funnel appears at the base of a thundercloud

1. Wall of cloud

These photographs show how a tornado develops. Its funnel descends from a thundercloud above. A column of cloud then forms as moisture as the air condenses in the low pressure inside the tornado.

Funnel changes color as it picks up debris

2. Down to earth

This tornado is passing over dusty farmland. The base of the tornado is therefore obscured by dust picked up by the rising air and swirling winds.

Funnel narrows as the tornado's energy diminishes

3. Losing power

Energy from the tornado's winds throws debris into the air. As the tornado loses energy, it slows down. The funnel will then shrink back to the thundercloud from which it was born.

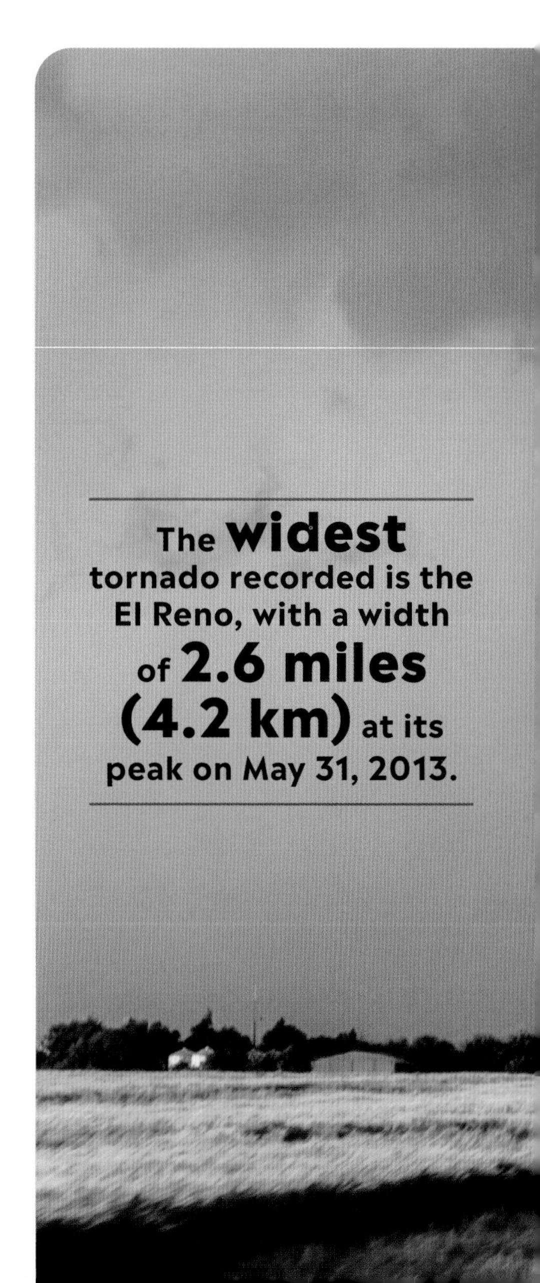

The widest tornado recorded is the El Reno, with a width of 2.6 miles (4.2 km) at its peak on May 31, 2013.

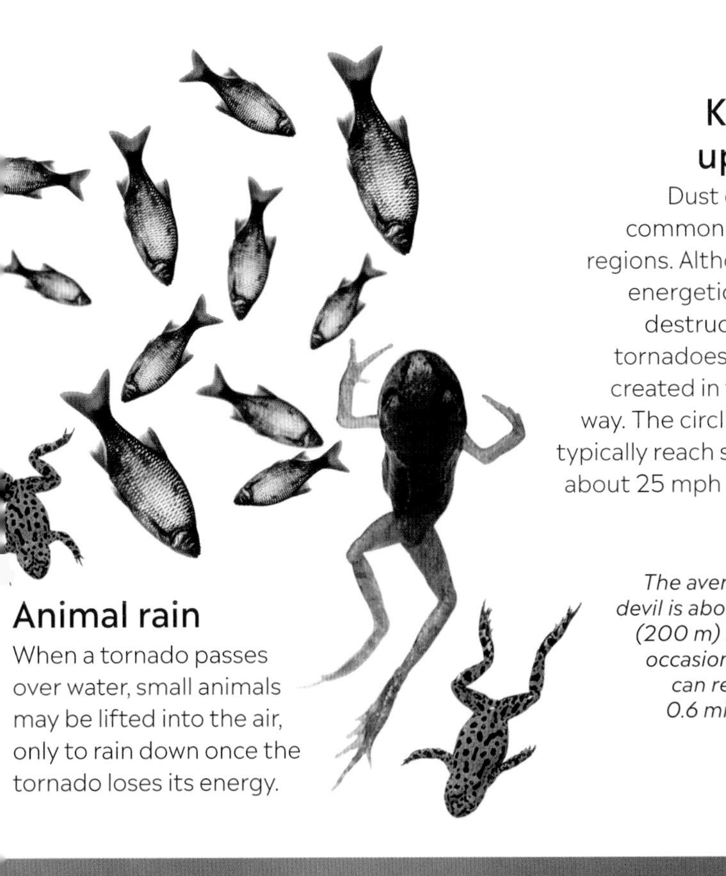

Animal rain

When a tornado passes over water, small animals may be lifted into the air, only to rain down once the tornado loses its energy.

Kicking up dust

Dust devils are common in desert regions. Although less energetic and less destructive than tornadoes, they are created in the same way. The circling winds typically reach speeds of about 25 mph (40 kph).

The average dust devil is about 656 ft (200 m) high, but occasionally they can reach over 0.6 mile (1 km).

Spin cycle

The writhing funnel of rapidly spinning air descends to the ground from the base of a supercell. At a tornado's heart, a low-pressure vortex acts like a huge vacuum cleaner, sucking up air and anything on the ground.

Swirling black thundercloud indicates the start of a tornado

Tornado **force**

The swirling winds of a tornado are among the most destructive forces in nature, with speeds of up to 310 mph (500 kph). A violent tornado will destroy everything in its path. Most of the world's destructive tornadoes occur during spring and early summer in the Midwest and southeast US, where cold air from Canada in the north sits atop warm, moist air from the Gulf of Mexico to the south. Predicting where and when tornadoes will occur is extremely difficult.

TORNADO ALLEY

The risk of tornadoes across the US is high in the eastern half of the country, with the highest risk regions in Tornado Alley (Oklahoma, Kansas, and Missouri) and in the southeast (Mississippi and Alabama). The US experiences more than 1,000 tornadoes each year, which claim about 100 lives.

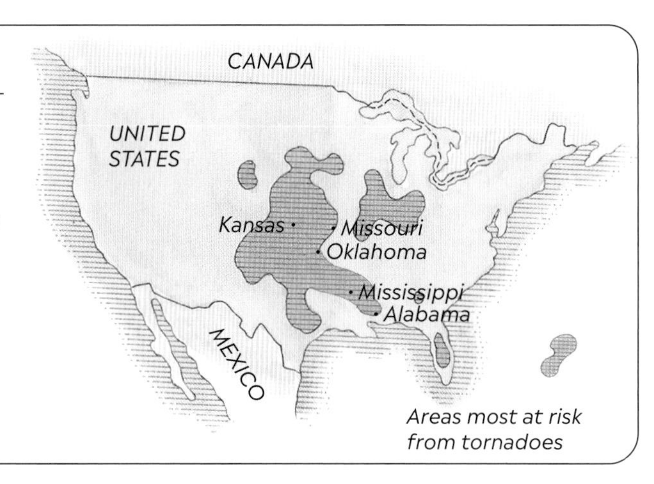

Towering

The destructive vortex (spinning center) of a tornado is usually about 1 mile (2 km) wide. Dust or objects at ground level are lifted high into the air and flung sideways, or kept in the air and deposited when the tornado winds down. Tornadoes typically travel at 34 mph (55 kph).

Blown away

In March 1994, a tornado ripped the roof off this church in Piedmont, Virginia, surprising the congregation during a service.

In a twist

Tornado winds traveling at more than 200 mph (322 kph) in Missouri picked up this car and hurled it down again, leaving behind a mess of twisted steel and showing the incredible power of a tornado.

The Daulatpur-Saturia tornado in Bangladesh is said to be the deadliest in history, killing 1,300 people.

Debris and objects such as this car can be swept up when a tornado passes over the ground

Storm chasing

In the US, storm chasers pursue supercells and tornadoes, mostly for recreation and thrill-seeking, but also to learn more about these powerful and destructive systems.

Blind panic

Much of a tornado's destruction is caused by the sudden drop in pressure that it brings. This window exploded outward when a tornado went by because air pressure inside the room was higher than outside.

Volunteer removing broken glass

Strange tales

A chicken in Alabama is reported to have survived tornadic winds of about 124 mph (200 kph), which stripped it of its tail and feathers.

EYEWITNESS

Early description

The first record of a tornado is said to be in a report by John Winthrop in July 1643. Winthrop was interested in studying weather and kept weather logs. He said he saw a gust of wind that felled trees, blew up dust, and even lifted a house in Newbury, MA.

Measuring tornadoes

Meteorologists use an anemometer to accurately measure wind speeds, but getting one inside a tornado is dangerous, and, because tornadoes move, it is difficult to get accurate readings. And so meteorologists categorized tornadoes based on estimated wind speed and damage caused. Today, though, the Doppler weather radar accurately measures wind speeds inside a tornado.

Path of a tornado

Most tornadoes travel at 20-50 mph (30-80 kph). This image shows the path of devastation left by a tornado in Oklahoma in 1999.

Doppler on wheels

Doppler radar, mounted on a truck to get close to the tornado, measures wind speed in a tornado without equipment breaking or anybody getting hurt. Microwaves directed at the tornado's edge bounce off water droplets carried by the wind. Computers in the truck then work out the speed at which the droplets are moving.

Radar dish sends out and receives microwaves

EYEWITNESS

Tetsuya (Ted) Fujita (1920–1998)

In 1971, this severe weather expert designed the Fujita (F) Scale, which categorizes tornadoes based on the damage they cause. Today, most countries use the Enhanced Fujita (EF) Scale, while meteorologists in the UK use the TORRO (T) Scale.

Tornado Intercept Vehicle

A tanklike vehicle called the Tornado Intercept Vehicle was built so a storm chaser could film inside a tornado using an IMAX camera. In Kansas in 2013, a strong tornado with winds measuring more than 150 mph (241 kph) was intercepted by the vehicle and captured on camera.

Enhanced Fujita Scale

Meteorologists in the US and Canada began using the Enhanced Fujita (EF) Scale, which runs from EF0 to EF5, in 2007. Several other countries also use it. It gives more accurate wind speed estimates.

EF0: Minor Damage
The 65–85 mph (105–137 kph) winds can uproot shallow-rooted trees and damage chimneys.

EF1: Moderate Damage
Moderate winds of 86–110 mph (138–177 kph) overturn mobile homes and damage roofs and windows.

EF2: Considerable Damage
The 111–135 mph (178–217 kph) winds can tear off roofs, uproot large trees, and lift cars off the ground.

EF3: Severe Damage
Intense 136–165 mph (218–266 kph) winds damage well-constructed buildings and can overturn trains.

EF4: Devastating Damage
Wind speeds of 166–200 mph (267–322 kph) can ruin houses and lift cars, blowing them long distances.

EF5: Incredible Damage
Wind speeds of more than 200 mph (322 kph) are very rare but are able to detach houses from their foundations.

Lightning **strikes**

Nearly 2,000 thunderstorms occur at any one time across Earth. Their most impressive feature is lightning, caused by an electric charge that builds up inside a thundercloud. Air inside the cloud rises at speeds of up to 60 mph (100 kph) and carries tiny ice crystals to the top of the cloud. These rub against hail pellets as they rise. The ice crystals become positively charged; the hail becomes negatively charged. A lightning bolt is simply a huge spark that neutralizes the electric charges.

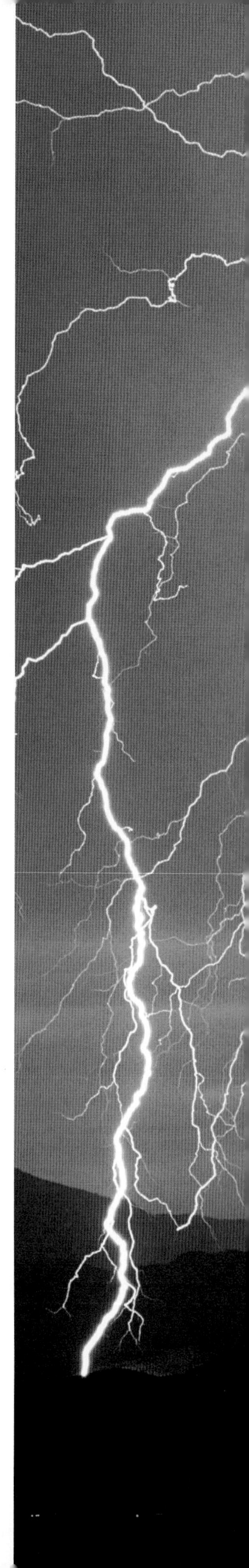

Sky lights

Most lightning bolts occur within a cloud. A powerful electric current passes between the positively charged top of the cloud and its negatively charged base.

Cloud illuminated from within by a lightning bolt

This tree has been torn apart by lightning

Lightning force

The power of lightning can demolish a building or kill a person or animal. Trees are vulnerable to lightning strikes, because the moist layer below the bark acts as a conductor.

Stormy god

Before scientists explained weather patterns, many cultures believed weather to be controlled by gods. The Norse god Thor was believed to make thunderbolts with his hammer.

Quick as a flash

Lightning, such as the successive flashes of this storm, begins as a "leader stroke" at the base of a thundercloud and forms a path of charged atoms. Electric charges race along this path, producing a bright glow and making the air heat up rapidly and expand. This creates a shockwave—a loud thunderclap.

Bright spark

During a storm in 1752, American politician and scientist Benjamin Franklin flew a kite with metal items on its string. Sparks from the items showed electricity had passed along the wet string.

Personal safety

The Franklin wire was invented by Benjamin Franklin in 1753. The metallic wire, hung from a hat or umbrella, dragged on the ground to divert lightning from the wearer.

Lightning rods were all the rage in Paris, 1778

Lightning rods

Tall buildings, such as the Eiffel Tower in Paris, France, are regularly hit by lightning. Metal rods (called lightning rods) attached to the buildings conduct the electricity to the ground.

Sand sculpture

This fossil is sand that has melted and then solidified in the path of a typical 54,000°F (30,000°C) bolt of lightning. The resulting mineral is fulgurite.

Fossilized lightning bolt

Hailstorms

Balls of ice called hailstones are produced inside a thundercloud. The strong air currents force lumps of ice up and down the cloud. With each upward movement, the hailstones collect another layer of ice, until they are too big to be lifted again by the up-currents. The stronger the up-current, the heavier a hailstone can become. Heavy hailstones can be life-threatening, but any hailstorm can cause damage. One of the worst storms was in Munich, Germany, in July 1984, with financial losses around $1 billion (£625 million).

Big chill

Large hailstones usually fall from "supercell" thunderclouds, which typically have a very strong updraft. These hailstones are the size of golf balls and fell in Montana.

Silver iodide and other chemicals are shot into the clouds to encourage rainfall and minimize hail and fog

Cloud bursting

To save crops from hail damage, people fire chemical substances into thunderclouds with rocket flares, making potential hail fall as harmless rain. This can save vast stretches of grain that could be flattened by hail within minutes.

Heavy storm

Hailstones are usually about the size of a pea. They bounce when they hit a hard surface and tend to settle on the ground. But hailstones vary in size, and storms in severity. In the US alone, a hailstorm can cause property damage of more than $500 million (£300 million) and crop damage of $300 million (£185 million).

Dangerous driving

Driving through a hailstorm is hazardous; vehicles skid on the hard, icy stones. The damage caused by falling hail depends on the wind speed during a storm. Hailstones with a diameter of 4 in (10 cm) travel at speeds of up to 106 mph (170 kph).

Crops damaged by hail in Hail Alley

Ice pack

Hailstones are made up of layers—a bit like onions. Each layer represents one journey through the cloud in which it formed. This hailstone—one of the largest ever found—had a diameter of 7.5 in (19 cm) and a mass of 1.67 lb (766 g).

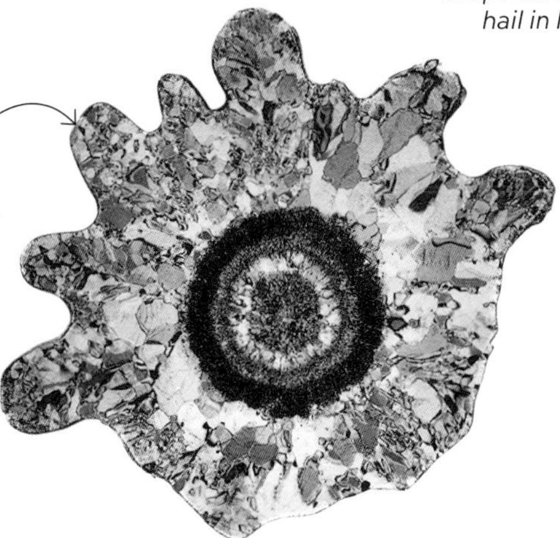

Cross-section of a hailstone

Hail Alley

A belt of land in the US, from Texas to Montana, known as “Hail Alley” experiences severe hailstorms more frequently than the rest of the country. Some researchers have predicted that due to climate change, hailstorms will become more frequent and hailstones will increase in size in the coming decades.

Warning

The destruction from a hurricane can be reduced if a warning is given. These flags are a hurricane alert.

Hurricane **alert**

Hurricanes, or tropical cyclones, are also known as cyclones in the Indian Ocean and typhoons in the Pacific. They are huge, rotating storms with winds of up to 217 mph (350 kph), heavy rain, and stormy seas. In the warm seas of the tropics (between the region about 5° and 20° north and south of the equator), a hurricane begins as heated air expands and rises, creating an area of low pressure. Surrounding air moves toward the low pressure and spins due to Earth's rotation.

A community in Bangladesh waits for a hurricane threat to pass

Safety on stilts

Floods are common during a hurricane, from heavy rains and high ocean waves. This shelter is raised so that flood waters can pass beneath it without endangering lives.

Stilts raise this specially designed cyclone shelter above the ground

Wheeled warning

In a Bangladesh village, where few people have radios or televisions, this man is using a megaphone to warn of a hurricane.

SPINNING CYCLONES

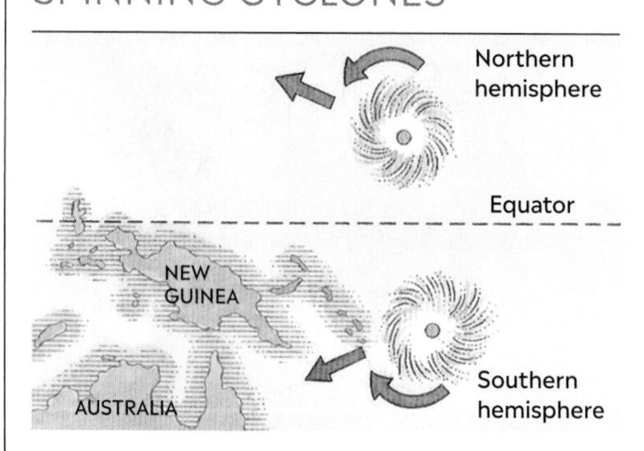

Hurricanes are tropical cyclones. A cyclone is an area of low-pressure air with winds that spiral inward—clockwise in the southern hemisphere, counterclockwise in the northern. They move west from their origin near the equator but may curve back east as they cross the tropics.

Water, water...

Storm surge is the abnormal rise in sea level during a storm, mostly caused by the strong winds of an approaching hurricane pushing water toward the shore. The sea level can bulge to more than 16 ft (5 m) higher than normal. This surge adds to the flooding along coastlines, which causes most of the deaths from hurricanes.

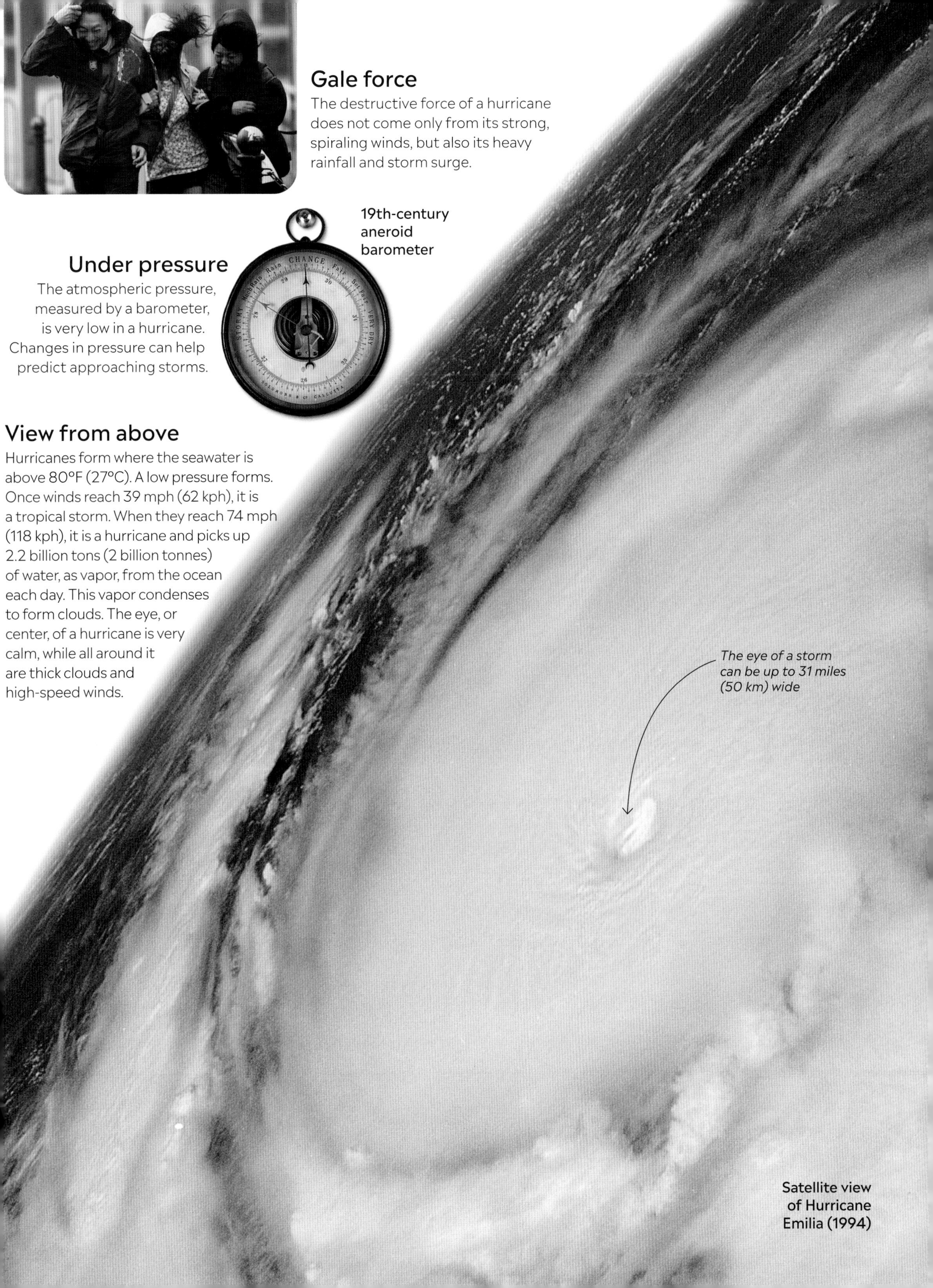

Gale force

The destructive force of a hurricane does not come only from its strong, spiraling winds, but also its heavy rainfall and storm surge.

19th-century aneroid barometer

Under pressure

The atmospheric pressure, measured by a barometer, is very low in a hurricane. Changes in pressure can help predict approaching storms.

View from above

Hurricanes form where the seawater is above 80°F (27°C). A low pressure forms. Once winds reach 39 mph (62 kph), it is a tropical storm. When they reach 74 mph (118 kph), it is a hurricane and picks up 2.2 billion tons (2 billion tonnes) of water, as vapor, from the ocean each day. This vapor condenses to form clouds. The eye, or center, of a hurricane is very calm, while all around it are thick clouds and high-speed winds.

The eye of a storm can be up to 31 miles (50 km) wide

Satellite view of Hurricane Emilia (1994)

Devastation

Some regions are more prone to hurricanes than others. Areas outside the tropics—more than 1,550 miles (2,500 km) from the equator—are much less at risk than tropical regions, because the seas are cooler, providing less energy to fuel hurricanes. Hurricanes bring huge waves, known as storm surges, which cause the biggest loss of lives. But it is the winds, persistent rainfall, and flooding that cause the greatest destruction.

Satellite image of Hurricane Maria

Hurricane Maria

The northeastern Caribbean, in particular Puerto Rico and Dominica, were badly damaged by Hurricane Maria in late September 2017. The deadly storm caused a major humanitarian crisis and became the third costliest hurricane in US history, with estimated losses of $92 billion.

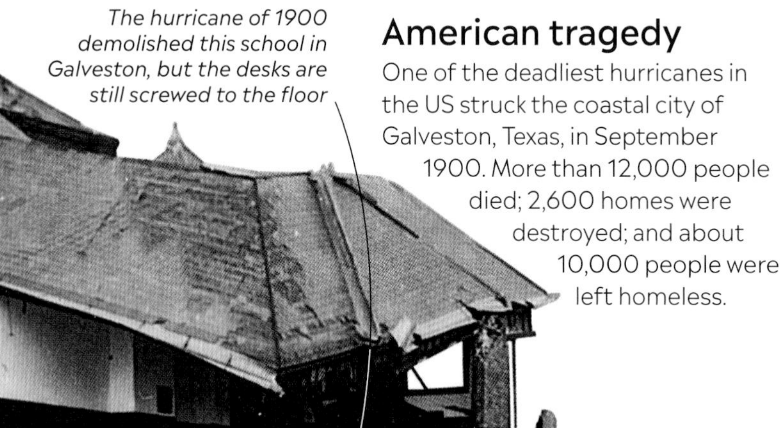

The hurricane of 1900 demolished this school in Galveston, but the desks are still screwed to the floor

American tragedy

One of the deadliest hurricanes in the US struck the coastal city of Galveston, Texas, in September 1900. More than 12,000 people died; 2,600 homes were destroyed; and about 10,000 people were left homeless.

Survivor's message

In August 1992, Hurricane Andrew devastated the Bahamas, Louisiana, and Florida. It caused 52 deaths and about $22 billion worth of damage. By writing on the roof, the resident of this house tried to say that the fierce storm had caused havoc.

Typhoon Haiyan

Typhoon Haiyan, known locally as Typhoon Yolanda, caused devastation across the Philippines in Southeast Asia, making landfall on November 8, 2013. The storm became the deadliest in the country's modern record, killing more than 6,300 people and leaving 4 million people homeless. The storm surge level was estimated at 16–20 ft (5–6 m) and was largely responsible for the destruction.

EYEWITNESS

Inspiring change

When Typhoon Haiyan tore through the Philippines in 2013, one of the worst-hit cities was Tacloban. Having survived the destructive storm and its aftermath, John Leonard Chan (seen here, right, with former VP and environmentalist Al Gore) became a Climate Reality leader to educate people against the perils of climate change and to work to reduce environmental damage.

Reduced to rubble

In April 1991, Cyclone 2B hit Bangladesh; 150-mph (240-kph) winds reduced homes to rubble, and a 20-ft (6-m) tidal wave claimed more than 140,000 lives.

Since the 1940s, hurricanes have been given human names, but between 1953 and 1979, only women's names were allowed.

Hanging around

The Dominican Republic was struck by dangerous and destructive Hurricane David in August 1979. The storm reached speeds of 172 mph (277 kph) and lasted two weeks, bombarding the coastline with huge waves; 1,300 people lost their lives.

Hurricane David's powerful winds lifted this plane and deposited it on top of a hangar

Hurricane Wilma, 2005, near Cancun, Mexico

Gusty winds

This picture shows the conditions beneath a hurricane's spiraling clouds. The high winds are caused by huge differences in atmospheric pressure. As the air spirals inward, it speeds up.

Hurricane **strikes**

It usually takes several days for storms over tropical oceans to develop into hurricanes. By studying how hurricanes develop, meteorologists can better predict which storm will become a hurricane, where it is likely to go, and how powerful it might be, helping emergency services better prepare and giving people more time to evacuate.

EYEWITNESS

Animals in peril

The Society for the Prevention of Cruelty to Animals along with other animal welfare groups rescued hundreds of pets left stranded and homeless in the aftermath of the deadly Hurricane Katrina in 2005. Many among the 250,000 pets affected were evacuated, some even by flights. Afterward, the PETS Act was passed in the US to make sure rescue agencies save pets during natural disasters.

HURRICANE FORMATION

Hurricanes develop above warm ocean waters. Moist, rising air causes an area of very low pressure. Surrounding air spirals inward and forms curved clouds called rainbands. In intense storms, a calm, clear eye forms in the center. Surrounding the eye is the eyewall, a ring of deep thunderstorms accompanied by the storm's most destructive winds.

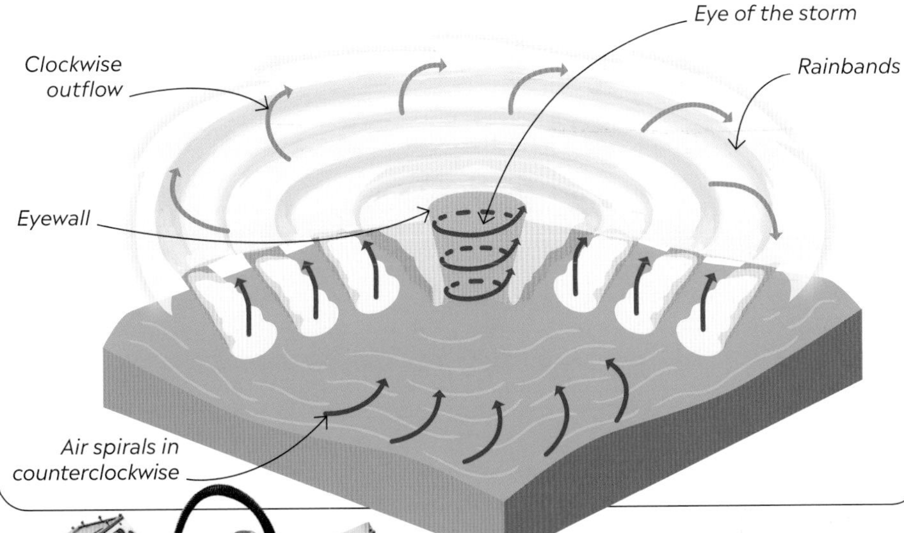

Hurricane reader

Mounted on aircraft that fly over storm clouds, the High-Altitude Imaging Wind and Rain Airborne Profiler (HIWRAP) uses radar to measure wind speeds around hurricanes, which helps scientists understand and make more accurate predictions about these storms.

Dish reflector

Two "transceivers" transmit and receive radar beams

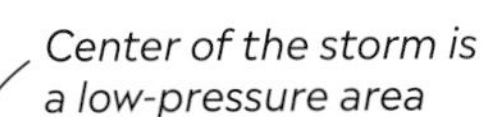

1. Hurricane trigger

These satellite images show Hurricane Harvey's evolution in 2017. After impacting the Caribbean on August 19 before moving into Mexico and weakening, the storm began redeveloping on August 23 in the southern Gulf of Mexico. A center of low pressure began drawing in air.

2. Mature stage

The storm absorbed more energy from the warm water in the Gulf of Mexico and rapidly intensified, becoming a major hurricane on August 25. Harvey made landfall at peak intensity over southern Texas.

The winds weaken as the hurricane makes landfall

3. Slowing down

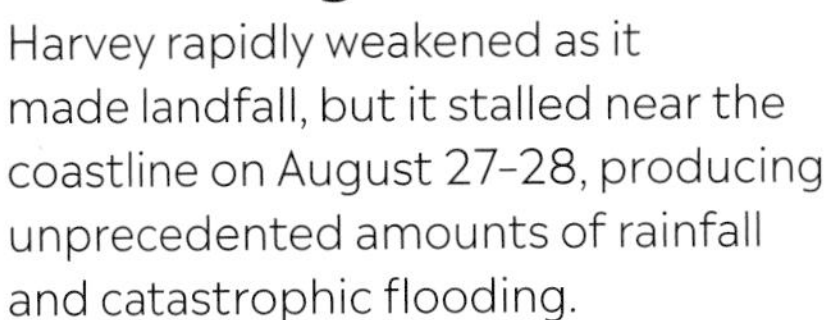

Harvey rapidly weakened as it made landfall, but it stalled near the coastline on August 27–28, producing unprecedented amounts of rainfall and catastrophic flooding.

Fog and **smog**

Fog is cloud at ground level made up of tiny water droplets. Fog is translucent, like tracing paper, as it scatters light. Thick fog reduces visibility, and accidents on the roads, at sea, or in the air are common. Foghorns or radar locate ships and planes; traffic signals and lighthouses can guide them to safety. When fog combines with smoke, thick and dangerous smog may form.

Mask protects policeman's lungs

Pea-souper

Until the 1960s, when the Clean Air Acts forced people to use "smokeless fuel," London, England, suffered dangerously bad smog, nicknamed "pea-soupers," from the burning of coal. It caused serious breathing problems.

EYEWITNESS

Water catchers

Scientists in Chile, including researchers from the Catholic University of Chile, built a fog collection system on the fringes of the Atacama Desert. Fog passing through large pieces of vertical canvas condenses into water, which is collected for farming, household use, and reforestation.

Take-off

During World War II, kerosene was burned to provide heat to clear fog from airport runways. The heat turned water droplets in fog into invisible vapor. It works, but it is expensive and can be dangerous.

Cleaning up the air

Sulfurous smog hangs in the air above many cities. It is produced when smoke combines with fog and is a danger to health and traffic. Today, sulfurous smogs are less common due to cleaner fuels, but equally deadly is "photochemical smog" caused by sunlight combining with air pollutants. Outdoor air pollution is responsible for millions of deaths each year.

Sounding the alarm

Thick sea fog hides boats from each other. Gas released from this foghorn makes a loud noise that can be heard clearly through the fog to help avoid collisions. Large ships have huge, deafening foghorns that can be heard over many miles.

Lighting the way

Before the invention of radar, sailors had no way of seeing in thick sea fogs. Lighthouses warned sailors of the dangers ahead, guiding ships away from rocks or shallow water, by flashing a powerful beam of light during fogs and at night.

Fog City

San Francisco, California, is known as "Fog City" due to its summer fog that occurs when warm, moist air meets the cool water that travels into San Francisco Bay from down the coast.

Tearing along

Crashing waves wreak havoc on coastlines, dissolving rock and breaking off parts of cliffs. The stormier and higher the sea, the greater the erosion. If sea levels rise, so will erosion and flood risks.

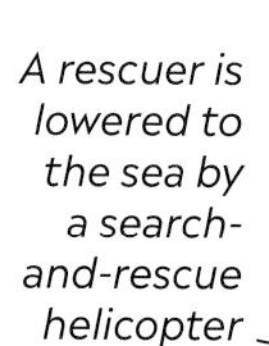

A rescuer is lowered to the sea by a search-and-rescue helicopter

In deep water

High seas have dangerous waves that can sink ships. Rescue helicopters help survivors, hovering above the sea while a rescuer is lowered on a winch to lift the survivors out the water.

High **seas**

Strong winds constantly disturb the surface of the oceans, producing waves that break on coastlines. During severe storms and hurricanes, seawater can cause flooding along the coast and ships to sink. Scientists fear that global warming may cause more of the ice caps to melt, resulting in a rise in sea levels, increasing the risk of flooding and coastal erosion in many places.

Stormy sea

Hurricane Hugo hit the West Indies and southeastern US in 1989 with a surge 6 ft (2 m) high. This rose to 18 ft (6 m) in some places, where the water was funneled up along valleys.

Tsunami

Often mistakenly called tidal waves, tsunamis are triggered by earthquakes beneath the seabed and can cause complete devastation as they move ashore, such as here in Sumatra, Indonesia.

Thames Barrier

The Thames River Barrier, one of the largest movable flood barriers in the world, aims to protect London, England, from flooding until at least 2050. Using information from mathematical models that forecast sea and river levels, 10 huge gates are raised when sea levels are predicted to surge, preventing water from traveling up the river.

Wall of water

Wind blows across the ocean surface, making the water swing up and down, back and forth, forming waves. When waves approach the shore, where the sea is shallower, they move more slowly, and their crests get taller and closer together. Eventually, the waves topple over, forming breakers.

This huge, plunging wave is on the verge of breaking

The tallest recorded tsunami generated a wave 100 ft (30 m) high in Alaska's Lituya Bay in 1958.

Snowstorms

Extremely cold conditions can endanger lives. When the temperature falls below freezing—32°F (0°C)—snow settles on the ground. Sometimes, wind blows the snow into piles, called snowdrifts. Snow and strong winds cause blizzards, which reduce visibility. Snowflakes are clumps of ice crystals made inside a cloud. Ice storms occur when falling water freezes on contact with the ground, creating a coating of ice. This is known as freezing rain.

Superstorm

The March 1993 "Superstorm," also known as "The Storm of the Century," was a large, powerful depression that brought severe winter weather to a large part of North America. Rare heavy snow fell in southern states, including Georgia, Alabama, and Florida.

White-out

Blizzards have forced these drivers to stop their cars. If they remain in their vehicles, they can be found more easily but risk freezing. One person froze to death during this snowstorm near Caen, France.

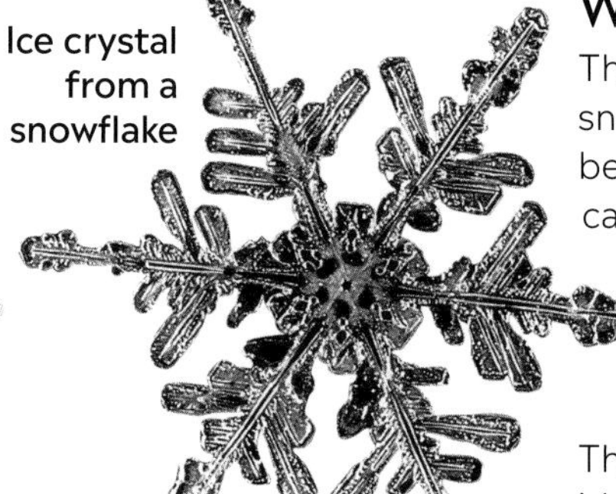

Ice crystal from a snowflake

What is snow?

The ice crystals that make up snowflakes are tiny, but their beautiful symmetrical shapes can be viewed through a microscope. Their growth depends on temperature, humidity, and air currents in a cloud. These conditions are never identical, so no two snowflakes are the same.

Blade of a snowplow clearing a road in France

Clearing the way

Snowplows keep major roads clear of heavy snow, and cars use tire chains for better grip. A sudden snowfall can cause chaos; tires easily lose their grip and accidents are common.

Staying indoors

Extreme cold weather can force people to stay indoors for safety and warmth. Vehicles may become frozen, such as this car in Montreal, Canada, when the temperature dropped to -5°F (-15°C) in 2017. This was the coldest day in Montreal in 100 years, with a snowfall of 10 in (25 cm).

Wind chill

Wind chill occurs on a windy day, when heat passes from your warm body to cold air more quickly than on a calm day, making it feel colder than it is. In January and February 2019, parts of the US experienced severe cold. Although actual temperatures were higher, wind chill made it feel as low as -60°F (-51°C). This cyclist's face-warmer froze on the streets of Minneapolis.

Frozen drips

Icicles form as water drips from ridges, such as rooftops or tree branches. A small amount of each drip freezes while the rest drips off. Gradually, drip by drip, an icicle builds up.

Icicles hang from a cliff during an ice storm in Arizona

Avalanche

One of the most dangerous things in mountainous areas is an avalanche, when huge amounts of snow slide down a mountain, burying buildings and the people in them. The Swiss Alps is one of the areas most at risk, with about 10,000 avalanches every year. Avalanches occur after snow builds up on mountain slopes in layers—a new layer laid during each snowfall. When the layers are unstable, an avalanche can be triggered by strong winds, vibrations, or changes in temperature. Anybody caught under this cold, heavy blanket needs rescuing immediately.

Bang, bang

When a mass of snow is ready, an avalanche can be set off by the slightest vibration. In places threatened by serious avalanches, explosives are used to set them off deliberately before too much snow builds up.

Snow fences protect mountain villages in Switzerland

Snow stoppers

Sturdy trees on a mountainside can absorb some of the energy of sliding snow. Artificial barriers made of wood, concrete, or metal can provide similar protection.

Under cover

In areas where avalanches are common, protective sheds are often built over major roads. The sheds allow avalanches to pass over the road, keeping the road clear.

Sniff search

Specially trained dogs help locate people trapped under heavy snow after avalanches. With their highly developed sense of smell, dogs are more efficient than any electronic sensor, although backcountry skiers do carry personal radio beacons.

A rescue dog searches for survivors in the Swiss Alps

EYEWITNESS

Predicting an avalanche

Scott Toepfer spent more than 30 years as an avalanche forecaster. He built snow pits to examine snow layers. Layers containing air or those made up of graupel (ice pellets) are more likely to have an avalanche. He identified danger zones by studying these features.

Snowy river

Airborne powder avalanches, such as this one, occur soon after a fresh snowfall. They flow like water, throwing up vast splashes on the valley floor. The high-speed mass of snow smothers everything in its path and compresses the air in front of it, creating loud tremors.

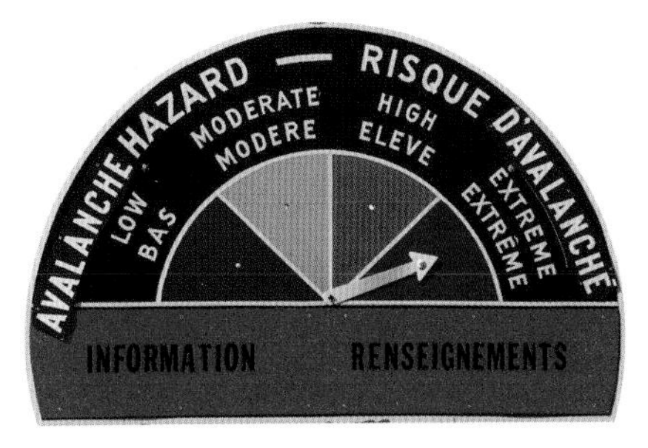

Watching for signs

Most mountain resorts warn of avalanche danger. By examining the snow, experts can tell when an area is at risk but not where and when it will strike.

This crack marks the start of a slab avalanche

Breaking away

Most avalanches occur when melted snow breaks away as a large slab. As it begins to move, cracks (fissures) show in the snow, usually on bulging slopes and snow that's overhanging clifftops.

Floods and **landslides**

Flooding causes more than a third of all deaths from natural disasters. A flash flood occurs when rain is heavy and rivers break their banks or sewers quickly become overwhelmed. In the Indian subcontinent, seasonal winds called monsoons bring torrential rain and floods every summer. When torrential rain combines with high tides and strong winds, coastal areas are particularly at risk. When large volumes of rainwater mix with soil, the muddy mixture can slip down a hill—a landslide.

Breaking the bank

During monsoon season, the Ganges River in south Asia often bursts its banks. The floods of July and August 1998 were the worst in 20 years, submerging up to two-thirds of Bangladesh. About 1,500 people died, mostly from snakebites or waterborne diseases.

Hurricane Florence

Hurricane Florence made landfall across North Carolina on September 14, 2018, as a relatively weak hurricane, and it weakened further as it moved inland. However, due to its slow motion, record-breaking rainfall coupled with a strong storm surge led to catastrophic flooding in both North and South Carolina.

Landslide

Torrential rain in Vargas, Venezuela, led to flash flooding and thousands of devastating landslides in December 1999. Between 10,000 and 30,000 people were killed, and entire towns disappeared.

Rice

Monsoon rains on the island of Java, Indonesia, are vital for rice crops. But sometimes heavy rains bring floods that endanger lives and precious crops.

A farmer in Java tries to save a rice crop from the floods

EYEWITNESS

Army to the rescue

After massive floods and landslides in Uttarakhand, India, in 2013, the Indian Army launched a rescue mission called Operation Surya Hope. They provided relief to thousands of stranded people and evacuated them from flood-hit places. Here, soldiers are guiding a group back to safety.

Surging waters

Cyclone Idai produced heavy downpour and a devastating storm surge of 14 ft (4.4 m) as it made landfall in the city of Beira, central Mozambique, on March 14, 2019, leading to flash flooding. Most of the city's population lost power.

Road damaged by heavy rains and flooding

Muddy river

In May 1998, after two days of torrential rain in Quindici, Italy, local rivers burst their banks. Muddy water flooded the town, leaving 3,000 homeless and killing about 50 people—many of them buried under a thick layer of mud.

Storm on the waterfront

These residents of the Florida Keys sought refuge as Hurricane George, which had already devastated Caribbean islands, hit the coastline in 1998. They battled against 90-mph (140-kph) winds and a surge of water from the Atlantic.

Home upturned by a powerful storm surge

The torrent built in a flash flood can sweep away buildings and cars in a matter of minutes.

Heat **waves**

A heat wave is a spell of unusually warm and humid weather. People can suffer from heatstroke—dizziness and confusion, nausea, and faster than normal heartbeats—which, in extreme cases, can kill. Sweating helps cool the body, but sweat evaporates more slowly in humid air. Despite the humidity, the land can be very dry, so wildfires are a danger.

Urban heat islands

Temperatures in cities are usually a degree or two higher (shown in this map as yellow and white) than less built-up areas, because concrete absorbs more heat than vegetation. As a result, people in cities are at the highest risk of health issues during heat waves.

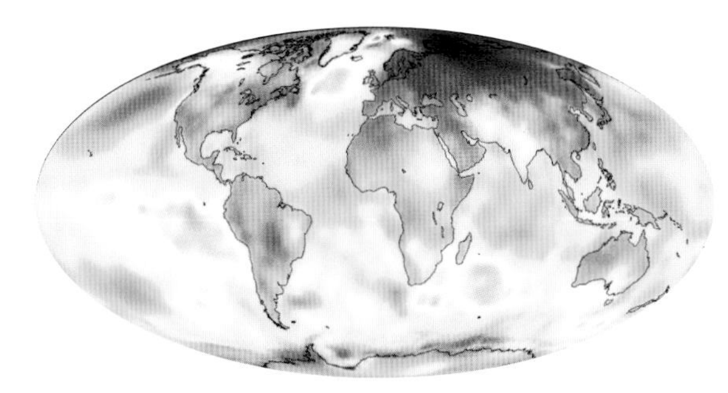

Climate change

Average temperatures are rising. On this 2020 map, orange and red colors represent regions where it was warmer than average; areas cooler than average are blue. As temperatures rise, heat waves are becoming more common.

Sun shade

During a heat wave, intense sunlight heats the body, increasing the risk of heatstroke and causing painful sunburn on the skin, which has similar symptoms to heatstroke. These people are using an umbrella for shade during a heat wave in Shanghai, China, in 2013.

Wildfires

In June 2012, the northwest US experienced one of its worst recorded heat waves. Record temperatures and very low rainfall created conditions for wildfires like this one in the heavily forested state of Montana.

A forest fire burning the side of a mountain in Montana

Moscow 2010

In the summer of 2010, much of Eastern Europe experienced record high temperatures. Wildfires raged for weeks in the countryside around Moscow, Russia. Smoke filled the city's air, causing smog—many inhabitants wore face masks, but the death rate in the city was twice as high for the month.

Europe 2003

People enjoyed the sunshine during the 2003 European heat wave. It was not all fun though: experts estimated that the heat wave caused around 70,000 deaths, and the accompanying drought caused crop failures.

Search for food

Heat waves can cause hardship for wildlife, as wildfires destroy their habitats and food sources. This deer is searching for food in a national park near Athens, Greece, after a heat wave in the summer of 2007.

Diminishing supply

Animals in dry climates gather around scarce pools of water, called waterholes. During a drought, more water evaporates and is drunk than is supplied by rainfall, and there are fewer plants for animals to eat, too. As a result, millions of animals can die during a drought.

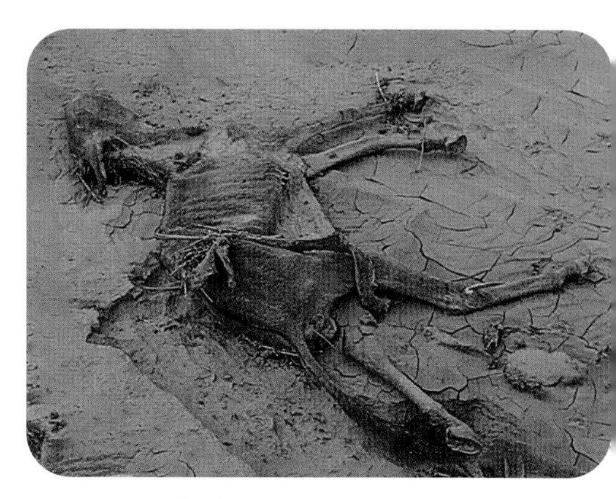

Skin and bones

Animal carcasses are a common sight during severe droughts. This unfortunate animal dried out before it had a chance to decay.

Deadly **droughts**

Any region lacking in water due to lower-than-usual rainfall is said to be in drought. As rivers, lakes, and soil dry up, crops fail and animals starve, leading to famine among humans. Advances in medicine, transportation, and communications in the 20th century allowed aid agencies to lessen the effects of water scarcity, but drought is still a problem in several continents. Droughts are sometimes caused by human activities, such as overfarming.

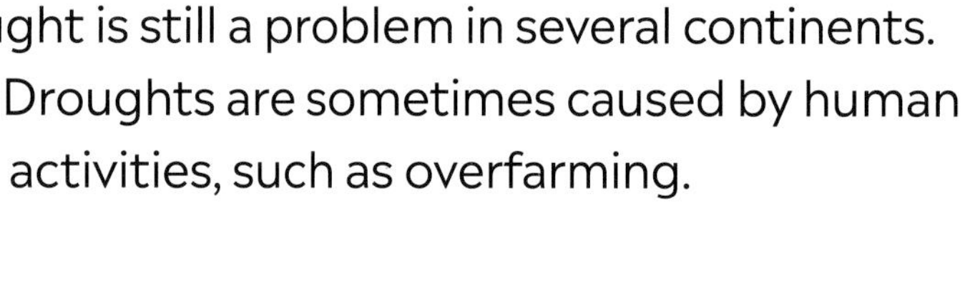

Cracking up

Large areas of land with no vegetation quickly suffer from drought. No plants means no water store, nor protection from winds that increase evaporation from the soil. Water helps bind soil grains; dry mud cracks up, becomes brittle, and produces dust.

Lake Naivasha in Kenya, Africa, dried up by a drought

Powerful painting

This Aboriginal bark painting is from Arnhem Land (a hot, dry part of northern Australia). Similar paintings were often used in rain-making ceremonies.

Blowing in the wind

Deserts are in permanent drought, so most are covered in dry sand or sandy soil. The wind can blow dry sand grains around, causing sandstorms. Sandstorms create sand dunes, which make up much of the landscape of the hottest deserts.

East African drought

One of the worst droughts of the past 70 years developed in East Africa (including Kenya, Somalia, Ethiopia, and Djibouti) during 2011 and 2012. After two years of very low and unreliably timed rainfall, crops and livestock were severely affected. More than 250,000 died, half of whom were children under 6 years old.

Fighting fire

Drought causes disastrous forest fires, fueled by the dry leaves and wood of vegetation. Most fires start naturally, but some are caused by a careless act, such as a dropped match. Some trees have fireproof bark, or bark that peels off when ignited. Other trees will not germinate until their cones are scorched.

Black blizzards

In the 1930s, the Great Plains of the Midwest suffered severe drought. Grasses in the fields had been plowed, so the topsoil dried to dust and blew away in clouds. Thousands left their homes, and some died of starvation or lung disease from inhaling the dust.

Thirsty leaves

In the drylands of southwest Africa, the kokerboom tree can survive several years of drought. Its leaves shrink, having lost most of their moisture.

Time freeze

Much of the ice at the poles has been frozen for millions of years. It preserves things that were around when it froze. By studying samples, scientists can discover what the climate was like many years ago.

Weather station

There are automatic weather stations across the polar regions. Forecasting the weather is important for the safety of those who live and work in these hostile environments.

Ice station

Polar research stations can house nearly 4,000 people. Scientists can learn more about Earth's weather patterns at the poles. As the Arctic is warming up twice as fast as the rest of the Earth, this weather research helps us understand climate change better.

Polar **extremes**

The North and South poles are frozen all year round, because they receive little direct sunlight. Around the North Pole, the Arctic has no land—only thick ice. Around the South Pole, Antarctica's land is constantly covered by snow. Strong winds in Antarctica are caused when cold air flows off steep slopes, blowing snow into a blinding blizzard. Temperatures peak at -40°F (-40°C) during the long, dark polar winters. The polar regions and their cold currents are important for global weather.

Wrap up

In polar climates, "extreme cold weather outfits" cover the body. Outer layers include waterproof jackets and salopettes, made up of several layers of different materials—the best way to reduce heat loss.

Undergarment traps a layer of air, which is warmed by the body

Bright-red color makes the jacket stand out in a blizzard

Elastic cuffs keep out icy winds

Get a grip

A thermal lining in climbing boots, and clipping pants to the tops, helps retain body heat in icy conditions. Crampons (spikes) on the soles provide grip.

Tough and durable plastic outer layer

Spikes help grip thick, slippery ice

EYEWITNESS

Experienced skipper
Born on a sailboat, Dion Poncet grew up surveying Antarctica with his parents. A ship's captain by profession, he has ferried scientists in the waters around Antarctica, guiding them in many explorations.

Poncet aboard the *Golden Fleece*

Weather balloon

Equipment in this weather balloon measures the temperature and concentration of gases in the Antarctic atmosphere. These measurements help scientists test theories and make more accurate forecasts.

Weather balloon for gathering data about the atmosphere

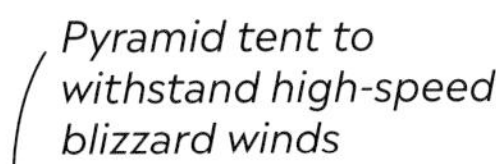

Pyramid tent to withstand high-speed blizzard winds

Fly the flag

Newly fallen snow and blizzards can bury important items. Some people plant colored flags to help them find their tents and supplies.

Eye protection

Goggles protect eyes from the glare of sunlight, which is reflected by the snow.

Waterproof nylon outer layer with goose-down stuffing

Breaking the ice

During winter, when huge amounts of sea ice form, powerful ice-breaking ships keep waterways clear, transport vital supplies, and are research stations.

Hurricane hunter

The meteorologists and instruments aboard this Lockheed WC-130 modified military transport airplane fly into hurricanes at an altitude of 1.9 miles (3 km) to help with accurate hurricane forecasts.

Weather **watch**

With enough warning that a hurricane is going to hit, many deaths can be avoided. Hurricanes can be tracked using weather satellites, but other types of extreme weather need ground-based measurements—including wind speed, temperature, and atmospheric pressure. The data are recorded using instruments around the world, on land and at sea. Forecasters use computers to analyze data and to predict how the weather will behave. The most difficult to predict are short-lived phenomena like tornadoes and long-term conditions such as drought.

High in the sky

Balloons are essential to weather forecasting. They carry instruments into Earth's atmosphere and transmit readings by radio. Measurements of upper atmosphere conditions are important for predicting what the weather may do next and for discovering more about how the weather works.

From far afield

This automatic weather station is in the middle of a field. It gathers measurements of wind speed and direction, temperature, humidity, and sunlight. The more data that meteorologists can collect, the better their forecasts will be.

Sea search

Buoys carry automatic weather stations. They drift in the sea for weeks, measuring wind speed, temperature, and humidity. It is important to monitor sea conditions, because they greatly influence Earth's climate.

Weather buoy

A large tailplane gives greater stability at low speed

Extra fuel is carried in tanks mounted on the wings

The world's first meteorological satellite, TIROS-1 was launched on April 1, 1960, by NASA.

Working with the weather

A modern weather forecast involves countless measurements of temperature, air pressure, and rainfall, plus complicated mathematics. Powerful supercomputers are needed, although humans are required to interpret the data.

EYEWITNESS

Joanne Simpson (1923–2010)

The first female meteorologist with a doctorate degree in the US, Joanne Simpson led the science team for the first space-based rainfall radar, the Tropical Rainfall Measuring Mission (TRMM). This satellite measured rainfall intensity and made critical inputs to tropical cyclone forecasting.

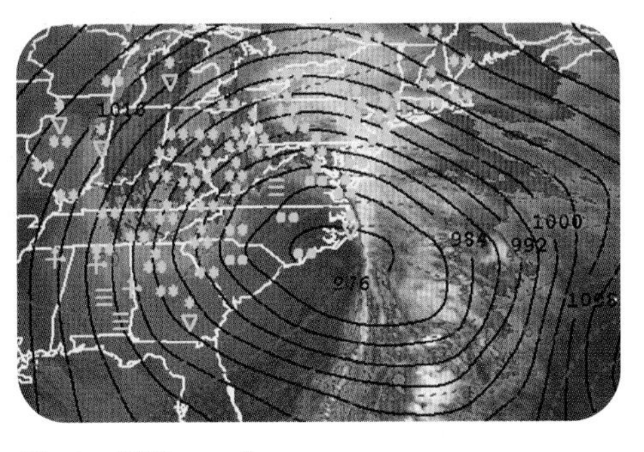

Satellite view

Infrared is heat radiation. It is not visible to human eyes but can be detected by special cameras. The warmer something is, the more infrared it produces. A satellite picture like this helps meteorologists measure temperature across the world's surface.

Round radar

Sensitive radar equipment enables weather scientists to make more accurate forecasts. The US National Weather Service relies on ground-based Doppler-radar stations to measure wind speeds and rainfall and calculate cloud positions.

Doppler-radar dome

Satellite is carried in the rocket's nose cone

There it goes

The Geostationary Operational Environmental Satellite system (GOES) is a series of satellites that monitor Earth's entire surface (except the regions close to the poles). This latest satellite, GOES-17, was launched on an Atlas V rocket from Cape Canaveral in 2018.

Disaster **relief**

Extreme weather phenomena, such as storms, droughts, and floods, can cause destruction on a huge scale. When it does, people may need help to keep them alive and well or somewhere to stay while their homes are being repaired or even rebuilt. Food and water supplies may be affected, too. International aid agencies provide assistance, food, and medical supplies to those who suffer due to the weather.

Air meals

When a natural disaster strikes a remote location, the quickest way to bring aid is to drop supplies from the sky. Each of the tightly bound parcels from this airplane contained sacks of grain. It is difficult to drop water in these parcels, even though it is often what is most needed.

Emergency food supplies

Upturned lives

A rescue team searches the rubble for survivors following a tornado in Oklahoma. People in central and eastern US suffer many tornadoes, but they can never be fully prepared. While rebuilding occurs, people are temporarily housed, possibly in a school.

Mopping up

A priority in a flood is to drain excess water. Powerful pumps clear the streets; sandbags protect properties from floodwater and control the direction of the flow.

Relief for people

After the catastrophe caused by Hurricane Harvey in the US in August 2017, aid was distributed quickly and efficiently, reducing the eventual impact on human life. Texas National Guard Soldiers arrived in Houston to help residents impacted by the hurricane.

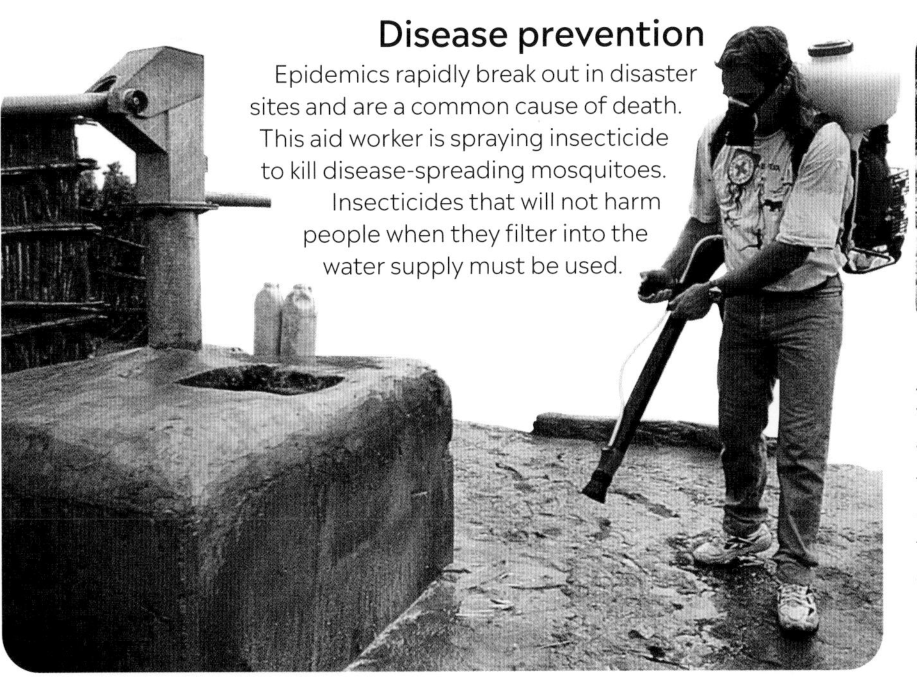

Disease prevention

Epidemics rapidly break out in disaster sites and are a common cause of death. This aid worker is spraying insecticide to kill disease-spreading mosquitoes. Insecticides that will not harm people when they filter into the water supply must be used.

All dried up

When this picture was taken in 2017, Somalia was facing widespread starvation due to famine. Famine is common during a serious drought, particularly in remote areas with few supplies. This is why food aid from organizations such as the World Food Program is important.

Makeshift shelters in a refugee camp in Ethiopia

Temporary homes

When drought brought famine to Ethiopia in 1989, the United Nations set up a camp in Sidamo Province, helping 45,000 people. Each family was given plastic sheeting as a temporary shelter, a sleeping mat, cooking utensils, food, and water. Refugees had to find their own cooking and building materials, putting a great strain on scarce resources.

Portable water

During a flood, drinking water is often cut off or in short supply. These children in Assam, India, are collecting fresh water from a hand pump.

In a cold climate

Emperor penguins live in the harsh Antarctic all year round. Waterproof feathers and thick fat layers help them survive on land and in the icy seas. During winter, their body fat provides an essential energy source.

Nature's survivors

The world's plants and animals are well suited to their environments. If they were not, they would soon die out, particularly in extreme climates such as deserts. Some living things are so well adapted to their surroundings that you may think they have been specially designed to live there. But living things adapt to their surroundings gradually—over many generations.

Some like it wet

Like all frogs, red-eyed tree frogs have moist skin. If their skin dries out, they will die, so tree frogs thrive in the damp rainforests. They also have suckers on their feet to clamber among the branches.

Feather coat

Snowy owls live in Arctic regions. Their soft, fluffy feathers hold lots of air, which insulates them against the cold. They even have feathers around their claws. If the weather becomes hot, snowy owls cool themselves by spreading their wings and panting.

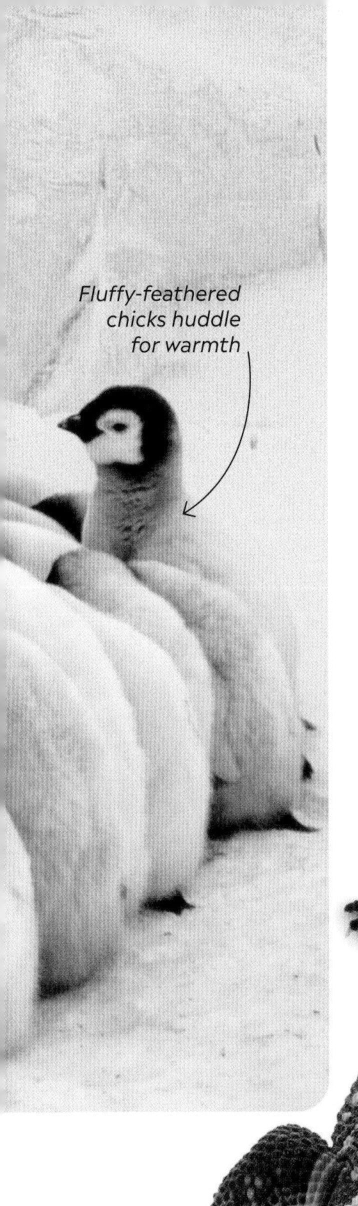
Fluffy-feathered chicks huddle for warmth

Useful tips

In a rainforest, about 3 ft (1 m) of rain falls each month during the rainy season. Plants depend on water to survive, but constantly wet leaves kill them. Some leaves developed "drip tips" to carry the water away.

Drip tip of a rainforest leaf

A camel can drink the same as a bath full of water in just a few minutes

Water hump

In the constant drought of the desert, a camel can make water from its own body fat, using a quarter of its body weight.

Fat stored in the tail provides energy in winter

Underground movers

Most amphibians need to keep their skin moist. During a drought, many stay in burrows or a moist location like a rotting log. During a dry season, some frogs become dormant, cocooning themselves in moist mud.

Australian burrowing frog

Fat monster

The gila monster lives in Mexico and the southwestern US. During the warm, rainy season, food is plentiful, and the gila monster stores body fat on which it can live during the cold, dry winter.

Stemming the flow

Leaves are covered with stomata (tiny holes) that allow water to escape. As it does so, more water is drawn from the soil by the plant. Where water is scarce, plants have fewer or smaller leaves. Many cacti have no leaves at all; they are simply large stems containing water.

Upside-down tree

According to myth, the strange-looking baobab tree angered the gods, who punished it by replanting it upside down. In reality, the tree has leaves for only three months a year, which, along with water stored in its huge trunk, enables the tree to survive East Africa's dry season.

The thicker a tree ring, the warmer the climate that year

Tree circles

Trees grow thicker each year. New living wood is created in a layer beneath the bark. Each year's growth appears as a ring. The warmer the climate, the more growth and the thicker the ring. By analyzing ring width, scientists can calculate average temperatures for each year of the tree's life.

Lost civilization

Dramatic climate change can force people out of their homes. The Anasazi civilization lived in these caves in the southwest of what is now the US until about 1280. They were forced to move by a 23-year drought.

Climate **change**

A region's climate is its typical weather over 30 years. But climates can change. Ice ages—when world temperatures are very low—cause more frozen seawater, larger polar ice caps, and more land ice in the form of huge glaciers. One cause of ice ages is the varying distance between Earth and the Sun. At other times, higher than normal temperatures have wiped out civilizations. Human activity, including the burning of fossil fuels, is currently leading to a rise in global average temperatures.

Woolly mammoth

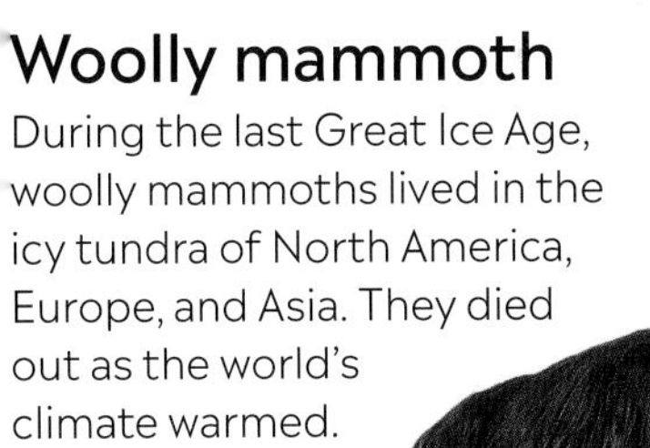

During the last Great Ice Age, woolly mammoths lived in the icy tundra of North America, Europe, and Asia. They died out as the world's climate warmed.

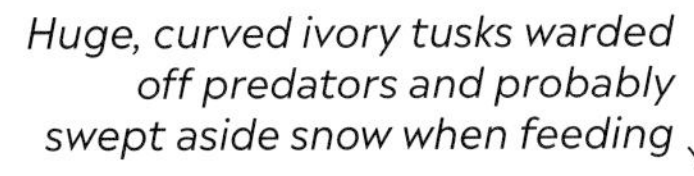

Huge, curved ivory tusks warded off predators and probably swept aside snow when feeding

Thick, woolly coat provides insulation

Living record

The oldest living trees are bristlecone pines, found in California and Nevada. Some are more than 4,000 years old and are a living record of the climate. Removing a thin sample allows its rings to be analyzed.

Ever-changing sea

The ammonoid, or ammonite, was a shelled marine animal that once lived in warm seas. Ammonoid fossils were found in Antarctic oceans, from when Antarctica was not at the South Pole, and so not cold. Like all continents, Antarctica has drifted across Earth.

Space dust

When a huge meteorite hit Earth 50,000 years ago, millions of tons of dust were thrown into the air and stayed there for a year, reflecting a lot of sunlight back into space. Some scientists believe this can cause reduced global temperatures.

EYEWITNESS

Young climate activist
Swedish environmental activist Greta Thunberg raises awareness globally about climate change and urges governments and people to take action against global warming. Her campaign began when she was 15 years old. She sat outside Sweden's parliament, missing school for three weeks, for what she called "School Strike for Climate."

Global warming

The world's average temperature is rising. Virtually all climate scientists blame human activity, such as the burning of fuels and intensive cattle farming. If global warming carries on at this rate, fundamental changes to large-scale weather patterns will occur, resulting in more extreme and frequent natural disasters and mass displacement of people.

Hot and cold

This map shows how El Niño affected tropical Pacific sea surface temperatures in 2016. The orange and red areas show warmer than normal temperatures; the blue areas show cooler than normal.

Seabed skeletons

Bleached coral indicates the presence of El Niño. Tiny algae live on coral and are vital to its survival. They move away when the sea's temperature rises, leaving behind the coral's white "skeleton." With higher temperatures, coral reefs become barren and die.

El Niño

Every 2 to 10 years, part of the Pacific Ocean becomes warmer than normal during winter, and Pacific winds change direction, blowing warm water east toward South America. This El Niño Southern Oscillation (ENSO), which can either be in the warm (El Niño) or cold (La Niña) phase, causes extreme weather in the tropics and can last up to four years. Outside the tropics, El Niño can cause average winter temperatures to fall and increased winter rainfall. El Niño can be predicted several months ahead, so early warnings allow farmers to alter their crops for the conditions.

Washed away

Much of the west coast of South America is very dry, because its coastal waters are normally cool. During the 1998 El Niño, however, rain began to fall at an incredible rate. Floods broke riverbanks and swept away villages.

Hard times

El Niño (Spanish for "the Christ child") was so-called by Peruvian fishermen because it appears over Christmas. When El Niño winds blow warm water over the cool Peruvian seas, plankton cannot grow in the warmer water, so the fish that eat the plankton disappear. Many Peruvians depend on fishing and therefore suffer during El Niño.

Steller sea lions are the largest of their kind

All dried up

During an El Niño, winds push warm water east toward South America and away from Australia in the west. The cooler waters around eastern Australia lead to reduced rainfall, and large areas suffer from drought, causing many farmers to abandon their land.

Heavy snow

During El Niño, the change in Pacific Ocean currents affects the US's west coast. Some areas may suffer floods; others become much colder, such as with the high snow levels in the Sierra Nevada mountains in 2017.

Warm and wet

The 2015 El Niño caused floods in Kenya, ruining crops and spreading diseases such as malaria.

Drought alert

El Niño reduces rainfall in Brazil, which can lead to drought. During the 1987 El Niño, Brazil's grain production fell by 80 percent. In 1992, scientists were able to predict El Niño, so farmers planted crops that would survive a drought.

On the rocks

Sea lions and seabirds off the western coast of South America often starve during El Niño, as they feed on the fish that thrive on the cold-water plankton. When El Niño hits, the cool waters are pushed down and the fish swim deeper—out of reach.

EYEWITNESS

El Niño researcher

Nicholas Graham, a meteorologist at the Scripss Institution of San Diego, CA, developed a computerized model of El Niño that can help predict the effects of this event on ocean currents and climate.

Magical snowballs

When new snow falls on old and is blown by a strong, warm wind, snow sometimes rolls itself up. It is rare to see them forming, but you may find a whole field full of spontaneous snowballs.

Colors in the sky

When the Sun is low behind you and it is raining, you may see a rainbow. Sunlight reflects off raindrops, bending as it travels through them. Each color that makes up sunlight bends to a different angle, so a rainbow appears as a band of colors.

Glowing globes

People worldwide have reported balls of light that hover in midair or drift along before exploding or fading away. This ball lightning is likely electrical, caused by thunderstorms.

Freaky **conditions**

Earth's atmosphere and the Sun provide all of Earth's weather conditions. Most people experience sunshine, wind, rain, and possibly snow, but the Sun and atmosphere can also create strange conditions. Many people have seen a rainbow, caused by sunlight hitting raindrops and bouncing back; few have seen a moonbow. Other tricks of light include halos, mirages, and the Brocken Spectre, while electric charges cause the aurora lights.

Colors at moonrise

When a bright full Moon rises in the east and the Sun sets in the west, you may see a rare moonbow. This forms in the same way as a rainbow, so the Moon must be behind you and it must be raining in the west.

Sunset spark

On a clear day, as the Sun sets or rises, a green flash may light the sky. It is visible only over a definite horizon and is caused by sunlight being bent and scattered by dust particles in the atmosphere.

Sun halo

When sunlight passes through cirrus (high-altitude) clouds, a halo can be seen around the Sun. Folklore suggests that halos are a sign of imminent rain, which has some truth to it, as cirrus clouds often precede rainfall.

Distorted view

Mirages are produced when light from distant objects bends as it passes through air at different temperatures, causing people to think they see shimmering, watery reflections in the desert.

Auroras

These displays of colored light can often be seen near the North and South Poles. The light is produced high in the atmosphere as electrically charged solar particles are attracted toward the magnetic poles and collide with air molecules.

Mysterious glow

St. Elmo's Fire is a rare light that glows at the tips of pointed objects during an electric storm. The glow may be caused when the point leaks an electric charge that is attracted to the charge of a thundercloud.

No two light displays of the auroras are the same— colors and patterns always differ.

A ghostly sight

Some mountain climbers see huge human figures. The figures are just the climbers' shadows cast on the bases of nearby clouds—an effect called the Brocken Spectre. The shadows may have colorful halos called Brocken Bows.

Beyond **Earth**

The Sun is a star orbited by eight planets and their moons. The Sun's radiation causes weather on Earth by heating the atmosphere. Mercury and many moons have no atmosphere, so they have no wind, rain, or snow. Venus and Mars do have atmospheres; some of their weather is similar to Earth's. The gases of Jupiter, Saturn, Uranus, and Neptune swirl around as the planets spin, forming spiral storms similar to hurricanes. Farther from the Sun, dwarf planets are far too cold for an atmosphere to form.

Scorching storm

The Sun is a ball of extremely hot gas, increasing in heat as you head to the core. The surface is turbulent: huge storms (prominences), caused by the Sun's magnetic field, throw millions of tons of hot gas into space.

Spinning spots

Jupiter takes less than 10 hours to make one rotation. This causes the planet's atmosphere to swirl, and the Great Red Spot (above). This spot is twice the size of Earth. It is a storm similar to a hurricane that has been raging for at least 330 years.

Venusian volcanoes

Venus's surface has volcanoes, similar to Earth. Most are inactive, but when they did erupt, they spat gases into the atmosphere that play a part in the planet's weather.

Running rings

Saturn, like all the gas giants, is nearly all atmosphere and becomes more dense the closer to the center you go. The planet is warmed by the Sun, but in some places, the outer atmosphere is still a chilly -310°F (-190°C).

Molten Venus

Venus is the hottest planet, shrouded in thick clouds of sulfuric acid. The atmospheric pressure at its surface is 90 times higher than that on Earth.

Icy Europa

One of Jupiter's moons, Europa, has a thin atmosphere made up largely of oxygen. This rocky ball is coated in smooth water ice. Some space scientists think liquid water might be beneath the ice, which means life could exist in Europa's seas.

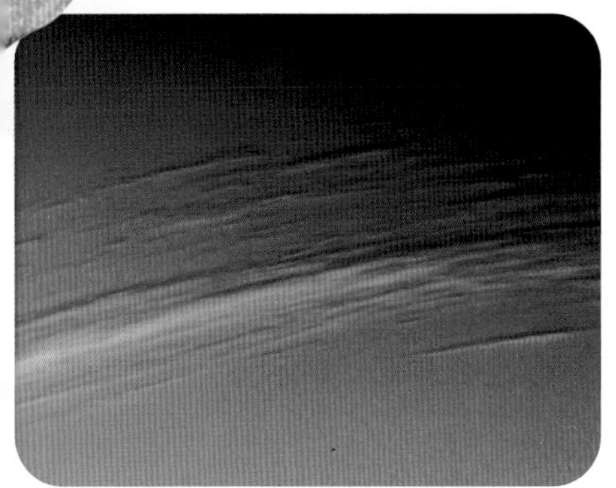

Blue Neptune

Neptune's 1,553-mph (2,500-kph) winds are the strongest in the Solar System. Methane gas in its atmosphere cools and freezes as it rises, forming white cloud bands (above).

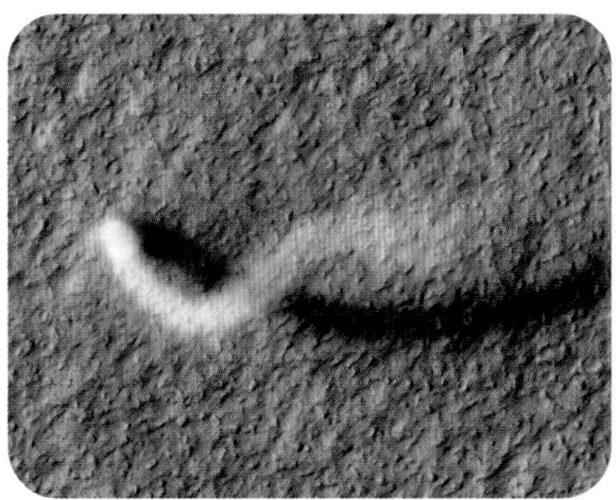

Dust storm

Mars is covered in dust that contains iron oxide—a compound in rust—giving the planet its reddish color. The atmosphere on Mars is much thinner than on Earth, but it still faces fierce dust storms. However, the strongest Martian winds are less than half the speed of the strongest hurricanes on Earth.

EYEWITNESS

Exploring giant planets

Planetary scientist Leigh Fletcher is an expert on the gas giants Jupiter, Saturn, Uranus, and Neptune. He studies their atmospheres, weather, and climates using information from observatories, space telescopes, and spacecrafts.

Did you **know?**

On July 7, 1841, hundreds of small fish and frogs fell with rain and hail on Derby, England

FASCINATING FACTS

A cumulonimbus cloud

Greenlanders have about 50 words for all their snow, such as "nittaalaq" (air thick with snow).

There are more than 8 million flashes of lightning every day.

Cumulonimbus clouds can be 9 miles (15 km) tall.

24 in (60 cm) of dry snow takes up the same space as 1 in (2.5 cm) of rain.

On August 14, 1979, a rainbow was visible in North Wales for three hours.

Thunder can be heard 6 miles (10 km) away from a storm, but lightning can be seen 60 miles (100 km) away.

A temperature of 40°F (4°C) could feel like -14°F (-10°C) if there is a 45 mph (72 kph) wind blowing. This is known as the wind-chill factor.

In storms, objects and animals can be picked up and dropped down again some distance away.

More than 100 tornadoes have hit Oklahoma City—more than any other city. Texas has more tornadoes a year—125—than any other US state.

"Male" hurricanes have caused four times more damage than "female" ones since 1979, when male/female names started being used.

Cheyenne, Wyoming, is the US's hail capital. A storm in August 1985 left 6-ft (1.8-m) high "haildrifts."

Permanent snow and ice cover about 10 percent of Earth's land.

A lightning flash moves from the ground to the cloud at 22,990 miles/second (37,000 km/second).

Hail falls on Keriche, Kenya, 132 days a year—more than on any other place on Earth.

Park ranger Roy Sullivan suffered seven lightning strikes in 41 years. It set his hair on fire, injured his chest and stomach, and knocked him out.

Lightning can travel more than 6 miles (10 km), so you can suffer a strike even if there is not a storm overhead.

Dramatic high tides result from high winds offshore and low atmospheric pressure. A 1-millibar fall in pressure causes the sea to rise by 0.4 in (1 cm); a deep depression can cause a 28-in (70-cm) rise.

A thunderstorm can drop up to 110 million gallons (500 million liters) of rain.

A tornado funnel sweeps across the ground

Fork lightning

QUESTIONS AND ANSWERS

What are the doldrums?

The doldrums are a windless area of rising hot air around the equator. The rising air forms cumulonimbus clouds that produce thunderstorms and waterspouts.

What causes the lights known as auroras?

Solar wind is a stream of particles flowing from the Sun's polar regions. The Earth's magnetic shield protects us from this wind, but at the poles, the particles create light displays as they collide with molecules in the upper atmosphere. Near the North Pole, the lights are known as the aurora borealis and near the South Pole, the aurora australis.

What is the blanket effect?

At night, clouds reduce the heat that leaves Earth, keeping Earth warm. This is the blanket effect.

What can happen where oceans meet?

Where oceans meet, such as off the tips of South America and South Africa, storms create huge waves. At Cape Horn, they can be 65 ft (20 m) tall.

The aurora borealis

RECORD BREAKERS

- In April 2011, the deadliest tornado outbreak in US history saw 358 tornadoes hit 21 US states in four days. Thousands were injured and 348 died.
- The all-time highest temperature recorded is 134°F (56.7°C), taken at the Greenland Ranch, Death Valley, California, on July 10, 1913.
- The wettest place on Earth, with an annual rainfall of 472 in (12,000 mm), is Mawsynram, Meghalaya, India.
- The wettest day ever recorded was at Foc-Foc, Ile de Reunion, Indian Ocean, where 71 in (1,825 mm) of rain fell in 24 hours.
- The windiest place in the world is Commonwealth Bay, Antarctica, where winds can average more than 50 mph (80 kph) at least 100 days each year.
- The greatest snowfall recorded in one day was at Silver Lake, Colorado, on April 14, 1921, with a fall of 6 ft 3 in (1.93 m).

Ice crystals in a snowflake

A surfer enjoys South Africa's big waves

Timeline

Hurricanes, tornadoes, and other extreme weather have caused terrible suffering over the years. This timeline charts some of the worst events over the past five centuries. Although we are now more knowledgeable about the causes of extreme weather and can better predict it, we cannot avoid the terrible destruction it brings.

A ship from the Spanish Armada

1495
A hurricane strikes Christopher Columbus near Hispaniola.

1559
A hurricane sinks almost all 74 Spanish ships heading to retake Florida.

1588
A violent May storm in the Bay of Biscay scatters the Spanish Armada ships on their way to invade England. The ships set off again in July.

1635
The Great Colonial Hurricane hits New England in August, causing a 20-ft (6-m) tide in Boston, destroying thousands of trees and houses.

1697
Lightning strikes an Irish castle, setting fire to its gunpowder store and causing the castle to explode.

1780
The Great Hurricane kills 22,000 (more than any other) in the Caribbean and destroys British and French fleets.

1843
A brutal hailstorm destroys crops and greenhouses in Norfolk, England.

1876-1879
A prolonged, severe drought in northern China kills between 9 and 13 million people.

1887
The Yellow River floods 10,000 sq miles (26,000 sq km) in China; 900,000 to 2.5 million people die.

1888
A hailstorm of cricket-ball-sized hailstones strikes Moradabad, northern India, killing 246 people.

1900
In September, 8–15-ft (2.4–4.5-m) storm tides inundate Galveston Island, Texas, killing 6,000.

Flooding on the plains of India

1925
The Tri-State tornado causes an estimated 695 deaths in Missouri, Illinois, and Indiana.

1928
The Okeechobee hurricane kills 3,411 in the Caribbean and Florida.

1930s
In the American Midwest, a drought turns farmland into a "Dust Bowl." Thousands die from heatstroke or breathing issues in the dust storms.

1930
A September hurricane kills thousands in the Dominican Republic and destroys its capital, Santa Domingo.

1931
The Yangtze River floods in China, ruining crops. About 3.7 million people perish in the floods and famine.

1953
A January storm surge of 8 ft (2.5 m) in Essex, England, kills 300, and of 13 ft (4 m) in Holland kills 1,800.

A storm surge rushes ashore

1959
A hailstorm hits Selden, Kansas, on June 3, burying an area 9 miles by 6 miles (15 km by 10 km) in hailstones to a depth of 18 in (46 cm).

1962
A massive avalanche and mudslide in Peru kill about 4,000.

1963
Hurricane Flora kills more than 7,000 in Haiti and Cuba.

1970
A storm surge floods the Ganges Delta, killing more than 400,000.

1971
Hurricane Ginger wanders the North Atlantic, the Bermuda Triangle, and the coasts of North Carolina and Virginia for a record 31 days.

1974
On Christmas Day, Cyclone Tracy strikes Darwin, Australia, killing 50.

1984
A summer hailstorm bombards Munich, Germany, with giant hailstones, causing $1 billion worth of damage.

1985
A million people are evacuated due to Hurricane Elena's erratic path across the Gulf of Mexico.

1988
Monsoon rains flood three-quarters of Bangladesh, killing 2,000 and making 30 million homeless.

1992
Hurricane Andrew strikes the Bahamas, Florida, and Louisiana, killing 65; destroying 25,000 homes; and causing damages of $20 billion.

1996
A tornado takes just 30 minutes to destroy 80 villages in Bangladesh, killing more than 440 people and injuring more than 32,000.

A giant hailstone

The result of mudslides in Venezuela

1974
Hurricane Fifi kills 10,000 in Honduras and destroys 80 percent of the banana crop.

1977
A tropical cyclone and storm surge strike Andhra Pradesh, India, killing 20,000 and making 2 million homeless.

1979
The 1,380-mile (2,220-km) wide Super Typhoon Tip is the largest recorded.

1980
A heat wave in America starts forest fires; 1,000 people perish.

1982
Monsoon floods in Orissa, India, kill 1,000 and make more than 5 million homeless.

1997
Lightning kills 19 people in Andhra Pradesh, India, on September 11.

1998
In May, a black tide of mud sweeps into Sarno, Italy, killing 130; 2,000 are made homeless.

1998
At least 2,500 people perish in an Indian heat wave in May and June.

1998
The Yangtze River, China, floods, killing 3,500.

1998
At least 2,500 die in July when a tsunami strikes Papua New Guinea.

1998
Two-month floods along the River Nile in Sudan make around 200,000 homeless.

1998
Hurricane Mitch strikes Central America in October; more than 11,000 die and 1.5 million are made homeless.

1999
Floods and mudslides in December kill more than 10,000 in Vargas, Venezuela.

2000
Torrential February rains in Mozambique cause the worst floods for 50 years. On February 22, Cyclone Eline hits, making it even worse.

2003
Europe has the hottest summer in nearly 500 years. More than 20,000 deaths are blamed on the heat wave.

2005
Hurricane Katrina devastates the Bahamas, Florida, and New Orleans. Property damage totaled $81 billion, making it the most costly hurricane ever.

2008
Cyclone Nargis causes catastrophic damage in Myanmar, with more than 138,000 fatalities.

2013
Typhoon Haiyan crosses into the Philippines, causing mass flooding and landslides. About 13 million people are affected and at least a million houses are either totally destroyed or damaged.

2017
Hurricane Maria kills more than 3,000 people across the northeastern Caribbean, including Puerto Rico and Dominica. It was one of the worst natural disasters in recorded history to impact this region.

Hurricane Elena

Find out **more**

There are many ways to find out more about the weather. Make or buy simple weather instruments to keep a log of hurricanes and tornadoes. You could look into projects that help victims of extreme weather or visit a wind farm to see how people harness the weather's energy.

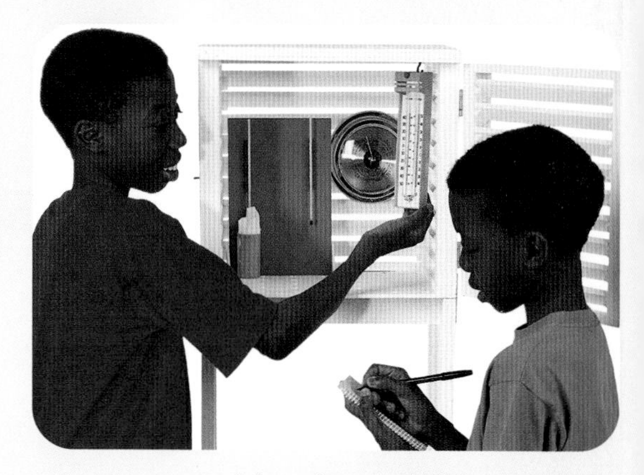

Monitor the weather

Build or buy your own weather center. Keep a daily log of weather measurements, such as air pressure, temperature, rainfall, and wind speed. You or your school could check out SciJinks online—run by the NOAA and NASA—to find out a great deal about weather on Earth and in space through articles, videos, and even games.

Visit a wind farm

Wind farms use wind power to generate electricity. Visit a wind farm and discover the advantages of this renewable energy resource. Find out where it is best to position the farms.

The blade turns to face the wind

Generator converts the movement of the shaft into electricity

USEFUL WEBSITES

- To find out about the National Weather Service, go to: **www.weather.gov**
- For information on setting up a weather station, see: **www.wunderground.com/pws/installation-guide**
- To visualize weather forecasts and weather data, go to: **www.windy.com**
- To find out about people who follow hurricanes, see: **www.hurricanehunters.com**
- For tornado information, see: **www.ncdc.noaa.gov/climate-information/extreme-events/us-tornado-climatology**

Hurricane crasher!

Find out how teams in the US and Australia track hurricanes to learn more about them in trucks and planes. They take photographs and measurements, and the planes fly right into the eye of the hurricane.

Stop the desert

Find out how people, animals, and plants survive with little rainfall. In northern Africa, drought, overgrazing, and removal of trees for firewood are resulting in the expansion of the Sahara Desert. Find out about the grass-planting projects to stop the desert from spreading.

Good flooding

Floods can cause damage, but they can sometimes be beneficial. They can increase soil fertility or create an environment for wildlife. The Ouse Washes, Cambridgeshire, flood every winter, attracting thousands of migrating birds.

About 7,000 migrating swans gather on the Ouse Washes each winter

Flood warnings

Contact the National Weather Service to find out more about flood alerts. Check out **www.waterwatch.usgs.gov** for flood information. Map your part of the country, marking flood-prone areas, and investigate why flooding is common there. Visit flood barriers, too.

PLACES TO VISIT

NATIONAL WEATHER MUSEUM AND SCIENCE CENTER, NORMAN, OKLAHOMA
This museum houses the original Norman Doppler Radar, which was instrumental in the development of Doppler technology and providing early warnings. You can also find an exhibit on how the weather affects food growth.
www.nationalweathermuseum.com

MOUNT WASHINGTON OBSERVATORY, NORTH CONWAY, NEW HAMPSHIRE
This weather station on top of Mount Washington provides hourly weather observations for the National Weather Service and offers climbing trips. You can also check out the summit webcams of different areas of Mount Washington.
www.mountwashington.org

MUSEUM OF LIFE AND SCIENCE, DURHAM, NORTH CAROLINA
Check out the 14-ft (4-m) tornado vortex that forms in an exhibit in the middle of the gallery and watch the climate in real time around the world on a globe at this museum.
www.lifeandscience.org/explore/weather/?utm_source=rss&utm_medium=rss&utm_campaign=weather

CAMPBELL SCIENTIFIC CANADA INSTRUMENT COLLECTION, EDMONTON, ALBERTA, CANADA
Here, you can find a collection of meteorological and hydrological instruments, such as rain gauges and anemometers.
www.campbellsci.ca/museum

Glossary

ANEMOMETER
An instrument for recording wind speeds.

ATMOSPHERE
The gases surrounding Earth and some other planets.

ATMOSPHERIC PRESSURE
The pressure from the atmosphere's weight.

AURORA
Bands of light across the sky, visible near the North and South Poles.

AVALANCHE
A fall of snow and ice down a mountain.

BAROCYCLONOMETER
An early device used to calculate the position of an approaching cyclone. It measured atmospheric pressure and wind direction.

BAROGRAPH
A chart with vertical or horizontal bars showing amounts.

BAROMETER
An instrument for measuring atmospheric pressure to determine weather changes or altitude.

BEAUFORT SCALE
A wind speed scale, from 0 (calm) to 12 (hurricane force).

BLIZZARD
A strong, bitterly cold wind accompanied by heavy snow.

CLIMATE
The usual, long-term weather conditions of an area.

CUMULONIMBUS CLOUD
A billowing, white or dark-gray cloud that is very tall. Also called a thunderhead, this type of cloud is associated with thunderstorms. The top of the cloud is often the shape of an anvil and the bottom can be quite dark if it is full of rain or hail.

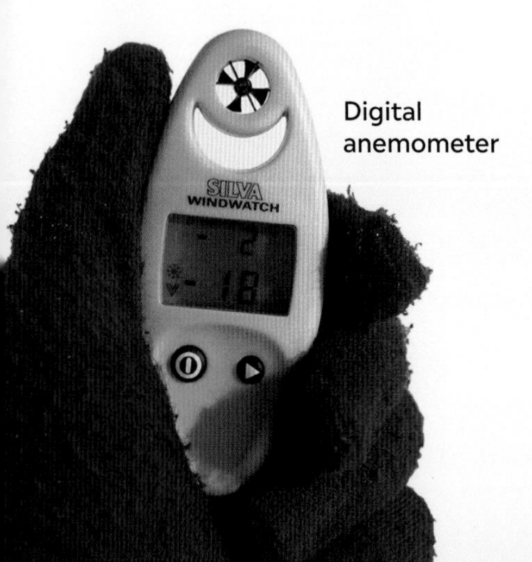

Digital anemometer

An early barometer

CYCLONE
An area of low atmospheric pressure with winds spiraling in toward it—counterclockwise in the northern hemisphere, clockwise in the southern.

DEPRESSION
A body of moving air that is below normal atmospheric pressure. Depressions often bring rain.

DOLDRUMS
Areas near the equator with very light winds or calms.

DROUGHT
A long period of little rainfall.

DUST DEVIL
A strong, mini whirlwind that whips up dust and litter into the air.

EL NIÑO
A warming of the eastern tropical Pacific Ocean, occurring every few years and disrupting weather patterns. La Niña, in contrast, is a cooling of the same ocean.

FLASH FLOOD
A sudden torrent, usually caused by a heavy storm.

FLOOD
When water overflows, such as from a river, and covers usually dry land.

FOG
A mass of water droplets hanging in the air and reducing visibility.

GLOBAL WARMING
An increase in the average temperature worldwide caused by the greenhouse effect.

GREENHOUSE EFFECT
The process in which gases absorb infrared radiation emitted by the Earth's surface, which would otherwise escape to space.

HAILSTONE
A pellet of ice falling from cumulonimbus clouds that have very strong rising air currents.

HAILSTORM
A storm in which hail falls.

HUMIDITY
Amount of moisture in air.

HURRICANE
A severe, often destructive storm, also called a tropical cyclone, and known as typhoons in the Pacific Ocean and cyclones in the Indian Ocean.

A meteorologist examines a rainfall monitor

HYGROMETER
An instrument that measures moisture in the air.

ICE AGE
A period of time when ice covers a large part of the Earth's land.

ICE STORM
When falling water freezes on contact with the ground, creating a coating of ice. This is known as freezing rain.

JET STREAM
A long current of air about 7.4 miles (12 km) above Earth's surface. Jet streams are hundreds of miles long, 60 miles (100 km) wide, and about 0.6 mile (1 km) deep. They can reach speeds of 200–300 mph (300–500 kph).

LANDSLIDE
The slipping of a large amount of rock and soil down the side of a mountain or cliff.

LIGHTNING
A flash of light during a thunderstorm, when electricity is discharged between two clouds or between a cloud and the ground.

LIGHTNING ROD
A metal strip situated between the highest part of a building and the ground to provide a safe route to the ground for the lightning.

METEOROLOGY
The study of Earth's atmosphere, of how weather forms, and of methods of forecasting the weather.

Under the Wave off Kanagawa by Hokusai

MONSOON
A seasonal wind, most well-known in south Asia. In summer, it blows from the southwest and brings heavy rains; in winter, it blows from the northeast.

PRECIPITATION
When water vapor condenses in the atmosphere and falls to Earth as rain, snow, hail, or sleet.

RAINBOW
An arc of colors across the sky caused by the refraction and reflection of sunlight through the rain.

SANDSTORM
A strong wind that whips up clouds of sand, especially in a desert.

SMOG
A mixture of smoke and fog.

SPATE
The fast flow of water in a river.

STORM SURGE
A dramatic rise in seawater level during a storm, caused by strong winds pushing water onshore.

SUPERCELL
A very large, long-lived, energetic cell in which the entire thunderstorm is rotating. Supercells create dangerous hazards, including tornadoes, torrential rain, and damaging hail.

TEMPERATURE
A measurement of how hot a body or substance is.

THERMOMETER
A temperature gauge, usually with a liquid column that expands or contracts in a sealed tube.

THERMOSCOPE
A device that indicates variations in temperature without measuring their amounts.

THUNDERBOLT
A flash of lightning accompanied by thunder.

THUNDERCLAP
A loud cracking noise caused by atmospheric gases expanding rapidly when heated suddenly by lightning.

THUNDERHEAD
A towering cumulonimbus cloud that is electrically charged. A thunderhead is dark in color, because it is full of rain or hail.

THUNDERSTORM
A storm caused by strong rising air currents, featuring thunder, lightning, and usually heavy rain or hail.

TIDAL WAVE
An unusually large wave not actually caused by the tides at all, but by an earthquake. Properly called a tsunami.

TORNADO
Also known as a cyclone, a whirlwind, or a twister. A tornado is a violent storm in which winds whirl around a small area of very low pressure. There is usually a dark, funnel-shaped cloud reaching down to Earth and causing damage.

TORNADO ALLEY
The name given to the parts of Kansas, Missouri, and Oklahoma that are most at risk for tornadoes.

Meteostat 7 weather satellite

TSUNAMI
A huge, destructive wave caused by an earthquake on the seabed.

VORTEX
A whirling mass of liquid or gas, such as tornadoes and hurricanes.

WATERSPOUT
A whirling water column drawn up from the surface by a whirlwind traveling over water.

WEATHER SATELLITE
A device that orbits the Earth and sends back data to help scientists forecast the weather.

WHIRLWIND
A column of air whirling around an area of low pressure and moving across the land or the surface of the ocean.

Flooding caused by monsoon rains in Vietnam

Index

Acknowledgments

The publisher would like to thank the following people for their help with making the book: Sheila Collins for design assistance; illustrators Eric Thomas and John Woodcock; photographers: Peter Anderson, Jeoff Brightling, Jane Burton, Peter Chadwick, Andy Crawford, Geoff Dann, Mike Dunning, Steve Gorton, Frank Greenaway, Ellen Howden, Colin Keates, Dave King, Andrew Nelmerm, Janet Peckham, Kim Sayer, Karl Shone, Andreas Von Einsiedel, Jerry Young, and Michel Zabé; Vagisha Pushp for picture research; Saloni Talwar and Priyanka Sharma-Saddi for the jacket; and Joanna Penning for proofreading and indexing.

The publisher would like to thank the following for their kind permission to reproduce their photographs:
(Key: a-above; b-below/bottom; c-centre; f-far; l-left; r-right; t-top)

123RF.com: mihtiander 55crb; **Alamy Images:** AC NewsPhoto 33cb, Agefotostock / William Perry 48tr, Art Directors & TRIP / Helene Rogers 46clb, Everett Collection Inc / © Paramount / Jensen Walker / Ron Harvey 31cra, FEMA 30br, 52cl, John Gaffen 63br, Bob Gibbons 24bl, Kelton Halbert 18-19b, Heritage Image Partnership Ltd / Werner Forman Archive / Museum fur Volkerkunde, Basle, Switzerland 6tr, IanDagnall Computing 21br, Ryan McGinnis 4tl, 21tr, Don Mennig 56-57b, NASA Archive 51cb, NASA Photo / Planetpix 51br, NOAA / Planetpix 33clb, PA Images 14ca, Pictorial Press Ltd 9tc, RGB Ventures / SuperStock / Weatherstock 10cb, SCPhotos / Bill Stevenson 40tl, Jim Snyders 60tl, StockShot / J Stock 41clb, Stocktrek Images, Inc. 33crb, Michael Ventura 51cl; Paul Wood 50-51t, Reven T.C. Wurman 22-23b; **Alison Anholt White:** 14tl; **Ardea London Ltd:** Francois Gohier 10bc; M. Watson 40bl; **Associated Press Ap:** 43tr, 43b; **Bridgeman Art Library, London/New York:** Thor's fight with the Giants, 1872 by Winge, Marten Eskil 1825-96, National Museum, Stockholm, Sweden 24bc; Plato and Aristotle, detail of the School of Athens, 1510-1511 (fresco), Vatican Museum and Galleries 6br; **Avalon:** A.N.T. Photo Library 19tr; **British Museum, London:** 7tl; **Corbis:** Aurora Open/ Patrick Orton 44-45b, epa/Paris Barrera 32-33t, Imaginechina 44cr, Reuters/Sue Ogrocki 22tl; **Corbis UK Ltd:** 41r; Bettmann 7tr, 25cr, 47cl; Lowell Georgia 4tr, 41tl; David Muench 56tr; Galen Rowell 40bl; Dave Bartruff 68l; Bettmann 66br; Rick Doyle 65b; El Universal/ Sygma 66cl; Chris Golley 64tr; Historical Picture Archive 71l; Aaron Horowitz 64bl; George McCarthy 69cl; Sygma 68br; Patrick Ward 69br; Michael S. Yamashita 71b; **Dreamstime.com:** Ajdibilio 57tr, Denis Belitskiy 60-61c, Delstudio 2ca, Constantin Opris 60tc, Peter Wilson / Petejw 47tl; Khunaspix 23tr, Lastdays1 23cra, 23crb, R. Gino Santa Maria 23cr, 23crb (Saint Louis), 23br; **Ecoscene:** Nick Hawkes 40tr; **Mary Evans Picture Library:** 25tc, 66cl; **Getty Images:** AFP / Bertrand Guay 50cr, AFP / Kerem Yucel 39clb, AFP / Martin Bernetti 34c, AFP / Mira Oberman 20-21c, AFP / Simon Maina 46crb, AFP / Simon Maina 59cr, AFP / STRDEL 42br, AFP / Tony Karumba 52tl, AFP / Zinyange Auntony 43tl, Barcroft Media / Anuwar Ali Hazarika 53crb, Patrick M. Bonafede 36clb, Giles Clarke 53tr, Corbis / Warren Faidley 4bl, 28tl, Denver Post / Andy Cross 40br, Denver Post / Helen H. Richardson 27cl, Andre Felipe 59crb, Handout / Lt. Zachary West 52-53b, Hulton Archive / Edward Miller 34cra, Image Source / Jason Persoff Stormdoctor 20bl, Los Angeles Times / Don Bartletti 59br, Chris McGrath 30-31t, Moment / David Hogan 2b, 14-15b, Moment / Ryan McGinnis 23cla, Moment Unreleased / Brett Monroe Garner 58-59t, NY Daily News Archive / Bill Turnbull 38tr, Tom Pennington 21cra, Reportage Archive / Philippe Bourseiller 48tl, RooM / kristianbell 59tr, George Rose 59cra, Science & Society Picture Library 9r, 15tc, Science Photo Library / Pasieka 12bc, Sarah Silbiger 57crb, Chip Somodevilla 42ca, Mario Tama 32br, TASS / Anton Vaganov 49r, The Chronicle Collection / Thomas S England 20cb, The Image Bank / Johnny Johnson 54-55t, The Image Bank / Warren Faidley 24-25c, The Washington Post / Whitney Shefte 1, 50bl, TPG 26bc, Universal Images Group / Photo 12 4cra, 13r; **Getty Images / iStock:** Marc Bruxelle 39t, CristiNistor 26-27t, Max Labeille 16t; 45tl, 45tr, AFP 45c; **Robert Harding Picture Library:** 11bl, 11br, 36-37a; Jon Gardley 49c; Dr. A.C. Waltham 36cl; **Hulton Getty:** Keystone 34cr; Painted by Stephen Pearce, engraved by John Scott 15tc; **ICRC:** Clive Shirley 53tc; **INAH:** Mexican Museum Authority, Michael Zabe 7bl; **Kristen Klaver:** 50bc; **FLPA - Images of nature:** J.C. Allen 27br; H. Hoflinger 18tr; NRC 27bc; R. Jennings 60tr; **Magnum:** Steve McCurry 42bl; **NASA:** 2tr, 2c, 4cl, 2cl, 28-29, 63bl, 62-63c, 62b, 62cl, 63c, 63cr, 63t; 17tr; Bill Hrybyk 33c; JPL-Caltech / Univ. of Arizona 63cb; **National Maritime Museum, London:** 8cr; **naturepl.com:** Kathryn Jeffs 49tc, Ralph Pace 58-59b, Phil Savoie 26c; Mike Lane 69cl; **Courtesy of the National Science Foundation:** 48tc, 49cla; **NHPA:** A.N.T. 19tr; **Panos Pictures:** Trygue Bolstad 46bc; Heidi Bradner 11tr; Jerry Callow 7br; Neil Cooper 47cb; Jeremy Hartley 46tr; Sim Holmes 2tc, 28c; Zed Nelson 28cr; Clive Shirley 58bl, 58c; **NOAA:** 58tc; **Rex Features:** 14cr, 42cla, 52bl; Jean Yves Desfoux 38cl; **Courtesy of The Rosenberg Library, Galveston, Texas:** 30bl; **Royal British Columbia Museum:** 57tc. **Scala:** Museo della Scienza Firenze 2tl, 8br, 8l; S. Maria Novella (farmacia), Firenze 8br; **Science Photo Library:** Roger Hill 18cl, 18clb, 18bl; NASA 44tr; Eric Bernard, Jerrican 38bl; Jean-Loup Charmet 25cr; Ben Johnson 36cb; Pete Menzel 25br NASA. 24c; Claude Nuridsany & Marie Perennesu 38cr; 57c; Pekka Parviainen 61tl; Fred K. Smith 17cr; Brian Brake 66tr; Cape Grim B.A.P.S/Simon Fraser 70r; Simon Fraser 70bl; NASA 67br; NCAR 67tr; Kazuyoshi Nomachi 69tl; Claude Nuridsany & Marie Perennou 65cr; Pekka Parviainen 64tl, 65tc; **Still Pictures:** Olivier Langrand 55cb; Hjalte Tin 53cr; UNEP. 61; **Stock Shot:** Jess Stock 10tl; **Shutterstock.com:** AP / Charles Rex Arbogast 14cla, AP / Dave Martin 43b, AP / Ricardo Mazalan 42cra, Cammie Czuchnicki 16crb, fivespots 55c, haveseen 35r, Nastiusha 17crb, Papava 40cr, Saurav022 34b, Mathias Sunke 46tl, Matthew J Thomas 36tl, TR STOK 12t, Xinhua 29tl; **Sygma:** 31cr; **Travel Ink:** David Toase 36tr; **University of Chicago**: 23tl; **Weatherstock:** Warren Faidley 4crb, 10c, 11cr, 39br, 51bc, 51bl, 61tc.